THE LITTLE BOOK OF AURA HEALING

The Little Book of

AURA HEALING

Simple Practices for
Cleansing and Reading
the Colors of the Aura

LAURA STYLER

**ROCKRIDGE
PRESS**

Interior and Cover Designer: Amanda Kirk
Art Producer: Karen Williams
Editor: Kelly Koester
Production Editor: Matt Burnett

Illustrations and photography used under license from Shutterstock.com and iStock.com.

ISBN: Print 978-1-64739-829-3 | eBook 978-1-64739-526-1
R0

This book is dedicated to all those
awakening to the truth of creation.

Contents

Introduction

Welcome to the beginning of your journey to understand, read, and heal your aura. The goal of this book is to help you achieve everything my journey into the unseen and subtle human energy field has done for me. It has allowed me to find a deeper relationship with authenticity, healed me from repressed anger and emotions, opened me to a level of receiving in relationships with others I didn't know was possible, and enabled me to experience myself as part of a co-creative governing force. It reconnected me to the light and innate wisdom of my soul that used to feel like a faint whisper and now is a powerful guiding force. With this book, you will awaken to your own personal power and find freedom within yourself.

In 2005, I attended my first aura viewing workshop as a last-ditch effort to alleviate the excruciating rheumatoid arthritis I'd been suffering from for four years. That's when my life changed forever. While doing one of the energy exercises, my partner in the class pushed energy into my aura. I felt a massive electrical current run through my body, leaving me with a deep, stabbing pain in my chest. Within days my life changed. I started seeing auras with my eyes wide open. Through the loving and compassionate structure of the Barbara Brennan School of Healing, I learned to see and interpret auras, heal the tear in my own aura that caused the stabbing pain, and embrace my latent ancestral healing gifts. I found a remission in the debilitating rheumatoid arthritis symptoms within the first two years of training. I went on to open my private healing practice in New York City in 2009.

This book begins with a brief background on auras and moves into specifics, including how the colors and chakras in the aura are related and useful for personal healing and fulfillment. We will move on to more detailed information and practices on how to read the aura. I have included a chapter on how to cleanse the aura with the most common tools healers use today, and we will dive into many different practices you can use to heal and strengthen your aura over time.

All of the information, practices, and tools in this book are an introduction for the beginner, with many expert tips from my personal and professional experience working with more than 1,000 clients and recording well over 10,000 hours of sessions over the past decade.

I hope this book is a friend and resource for you to check back in with time and time again on your healing journey. It is designed to build a foundation for your desire to know yourself more fully and explore the world around you with a compassionate viewpoint for others.

With deep love and gratitude,
Laura

CHAPTER ONE

AN INTRODUCTION TO AURAS

In this chapter you will learn what the aura is, how it connects to your everyday experiences, and why it's important to your physical, emotional, mental, and spiritual health. We will explore the layers of your aura and what each one feels like. You will discover which layers you notice most often and which layers you may want to bring more attention to for greater health and well-being. This information will be useful as you move into the aura healing and cleansing chapters of this book.

What Is an Aura?

A luminous energy field emanates from and envelopes the bodies of all living things. This electromagnetic field that surrounds our physical body is most often referred to as the aura or the auric field. Modern healers call it the "human aura" or "human energy field." It is more complex than the human body's physiology and anatomy. It contains all of your physical vitality, emotions, thoughts, and experiences related to others and with the spiritual. Your aura allows you to receive life's experiences on multiple layers of existence and to express yourself dynamically.

The aura has an oval shape like an egg. This outer boundary is strong yet flexible. The aura is made up of structured and fluid layers that hold and support each other, much like the way bones and muscles function in our physical body. There are many layers to the aura, and in this chapter, we will explore in great detail the main seven.

A healthy aura has symmetry front to back and side to side, with clear edges and defined boundaries as a whole and between each layer. It has vibrant colors that dance and flicker as well as defined grids of color that create structure for the energy to flow through. The outer ring typically extends one foot above the head and into the Earth and expands at arm's length from the center of the body.

The Aura's Origins

Throughout human history, mystics, scholars, and healers have searched to understand the formation of spirit into matter and to describe the unseen higher spiritual energy around a person. Civilization's earliest sacred writings refer to the aura and life force energy, the Vedas, from which the healing methodologies of Ayurveda were born. Both Ayurveda and Traditional Chinese Medicine have written descriptions and clearly detailed maps of the channels and currents of energy running through the physical body, along with entire treatment protocols. One of these systems—acupuncture—is still used today.

Many sacred traditions and ceremonies passed down through generations around the world include practices on how to cleanse the aura of negative energies and receive energy and support from the spirit world. Halos of light and energy around the heads of buddhas, prophets, and holy people appear in the artwork of many cultures throughout history. Additionally, Latin and Greek languages used the word *aura* to describe the air, the presence of someone or something, or a cool breeze.

Experiments in the 1800s and 1900s brought about the development of aura photography and the beginning of our ability to detect the layers of the aura outside the human body. From this, the movement of modern energy healing and self-development was born.

Aura Healing

Modern science has developed instruments sensitive enough to prove what ancient healing arts like acupuncture have relied on for centuries: that we are a field of energy with channels running through us and into our organs, down through every cell in our body. We take in energy from the ether around us through major power centers called chakras, which allow us to experience a vital and intimate connection to the world.

This book presents a variety of ways you can care for your aura and how professional aura healing methods support and bring balance to your energy. All aura healing methods are beneficial to the human energy field in one of three main areas: absorbing, strengthening, and cleansing.

- **Absorbing energy into the aura:** A variety of breathing techniques, meditations, visualizations, and movement exercises can be used to access the energy around you and within you and to harness it by drawing it in and moving it to areas where it is most needed. Channeling positive energy from your higher chakras and the people and places around you is a common way to increase the energy in your aura. You will find tips and suggestions about this throughout this book.

- **Strengthening the aura:** We lose energy from things we avoid, like when we avoid feeling certain emotions, and also from common daily stressors. Many forms of aura healing seek to replenish lost energy and restore balance between areas in your aura that have excess energy or a lack of energy.

- **Cleansing the aura:** An important part of our aura health includes removing old energies, energy blocks, emotions, and belief systems we have outgrown. Cleansing your aura, home, and workspaces from negative energies helps uplift and restore you and provides greater depth and understanding of your true self. There are many tools, techniques, and rituals in chapter 5 that will help you with this.

SUBTLE BODIES

Subtle energy and *subtle energy bodies* are terms used to speak about the aura, aura layers, and energies that we cannot physically feel or see but can sense. You are continuously perceiving subtle energy around you on a daily basis and are reacting to it before your conscious mind can register it.

You respond to energy instinctively without thinking because you are attuned to it. How do you decide if a person you just met is trustworthy? How did you know who was calling before you picked up the phone? Sensing subtle energy is interwoven in our language. We talk about the feeling of being "gutted" or "sucker punched" when hearing difficult news. We might say, "I feel heartbroken" or "I feel crushed" when we experience loss. We talk about feeling "scattered" or "drained of energy." These are some of the ways you perceive subtle energy through different layers of your aura beyond your conscious thoughts.

The Importance of a Balanced Aura

Your thoughts, emotions, intentions, and actions create and give off energy, which can be felt by others. When they are balanced, you give off a resonant or magnetic energy and others enjoy being in your presence. If these areas are discon-nected, others will have a feeling of dissonance around you and will not know how to genuinely connect with you.

The more symmetry in the size and shape of your aura and uniformity between the layers of your aura, the healthier and more integrated you will be in all areas of your life. When a layer of the aura is thicker than the others, this means the person predominately uses this layer to interface with the world around them. These are the areas where you will find your strengths and what feels most natural for you. Most people typically use only one or two layers of their aura to relate to the world around them, leading to a lack of perspectives and experiences of their whole self. Bringing awareness to the areas that feel more like a struggle or a challenge creates openings to experience other layers of human experience and balance the relationship between the layers of the aura.

Signs of an Imbalanced Aura

Have you ever felt like you had too much energy in your head, as if your head were way up in the clouds or cut off from your body? Maybe you have cycles when you feel really strong only to suddenly tank and crash? These are some of the most common descriptions my clients share with me when their auras have imbalanced energy.

We are constantly moving our energy in ways that bring balance or imbalance to our auric field. We can project our energy outward toward something, or we might squish our energy inward to protect ourselves from something. Emotional upheaval, or feeling scattered, is the experience of your energy moving outward in multiple directions. Over time, this can cause issues like anxiety, built-up anger, stress, depression, heartache, and depletion of energy, which can lead to illness.

You will find tools, tips, and practices throughout this book on how to work with these imbalances by cleansing your aura and maintaining its health and strength.

UCLA Study Confirms Aura Layers and Color Frequencies

One of the most influential studies of the auric field was recorded by Dr. Valerie Hunt in 1988 with well-known healer and psychic Reverend Rosalyn Bruyere. Electrodes were placed on a subject receiving a Rolfing treatment (a type of massage to correct alignment) while machines documented the wave patterns of low-voltage signals associated with color frequencies running through the body. Bruyere was simultaneously recorded while stating the colors she perceived moving in the subject's aura during the session. The results from the reports were consistent—the wave patterns corresponded with the colors Bruyere described seeing at the same time.

The Seven Layers of the Aura

Learning about the seven main layers of the aura and their relationship to each other will help you grasp the basic structure of the aura and get a good sense of how it works.

The seven layers of the aura are arranged one inside the other. The layers of the aura vary in vibration, which allows them to coexist while occupying the same space. This has been referred to by many healers as "nesting" or "cupping," like Russian matryoshka dolls. Each layer of the aura corresponds with a chakra and is associated with a color, which we will discuss more in chapters 2 and 3.

The vibration of each layer increases the farther it moves outward from the body. Each is connected to a different aspect of human

ETHERIC LAYER

EMOTIONAL LAYER

MENTAL LAYER

ASTRAL LAYER

experience: physical (first), emotional (second), mental (third), relational (fourth), expression (fifth), connection (sixth), and spiritual (seventh). These aura layers share information with each other, the physical body, and the external environment.

When your aura is expanded and open, it extends out to about the edge of your fingertips when your arms are extended. If you were to raise your arms up and out, sweeping them around your body in a circle, you would feel the circumference of your aura around you.

This is your personal energy space, your domain in which you have all of your energy, emotions, thoughts, and experiences just for you. Now let's take some time to explore each layer of the human aura.

ETHERIC TEMPLATE LAYER

CELESTIAL LAYER

KETHERIC TEMPLATE LAYER

THE ETHERIC LAYER

LAYER: First

CHAKRA: Root

COLOR: Light Blue to Dark Blue

SIZE: 0.5 to 2 inches from the body

The etheric layer is the first layer of the aura and is closest to the body. It vibrates at the frequency of physical survival and vitality. This layer creates and forms the foundational structure from which the physical body and human aura grow. This layer is connected to the root chakra and takes care of health, vitality, and structure for the flow of your life force energy.

The energy channels called acupuncture meridians, nadis, and major and minor chakras are located within the structure of the etheric layer. They are part of the structure that allows the flow of life force energy, called chi in Traditional Chinese Medicine, to be distributed throughout the entire aura and physical body.

Being the closest layer to the body, it is the densest of the vibrations of the aura. Though the waves moving at this layer are the slowest, they still have a higher vibration than the human body. This layer can be a whitish-blue to dark blue in color depending on the person's composition. It typically extends half an inch to two inches from the body.

A strong etheric layer is connected to good physical health. For individuals with a strong first layer of the field, it is much harder for them to get sick. If they have other issues on other layers of the field, they do not tend to affect their physical body as much.

The etheric layer is where you experience your willingness to be alive. This layer is connected to physical pain and physical pleasure. A healthy auric field pulsates in cycles about every 20 seconds, though it is slower in people with less vitality. Very sick people will have a much weaker etheric layer and a very slow "energy pulse."

Think of a time when you felt most alive. This will instantly bring you into the experience of the etheric layer of your aura.

THE EMOTIONAL LAYER

LAYER: Second

CHAKRA: Sacral

COLOR: All Chakra Colors (Red, Orange, Yellow, Green, Blue, Indigo, White)

SIZE: 1 to 3 inches from the body

The emotional layer is the second layer of the aura, which extends one to three inches from the body and is connected to the sacral chakra. It lies on top of the etheric layer and vibrates one level higher, at the frequency of emotions and feelings about yourself. This is the rainbow layer of the aura we are most familiar with. All of the chakra systems we see today present the aura in the bright primary colors of the emotional layer. These are red, orange, yellow, green, blue, indigo, and white.

The emotional layer is not physically structured like the etheric layer. It looks like a watercolor painting, with colorful splashes of clouds, fluctuating and moving depending on what you are feeling in the moment. This is the layer of the aura in which you experience your full range of emotions. Emotions can have a strong effect on the physical body, even causing pain and dis-comfort when they are held in and not expressed, because of their proximity to the physical body.

The primary colors of the emotional layer are vibrant in people who have clarity and openness. They are darker and muddied in people who hold back their expression or dim their feelings. You will find all the different colors connected to emotions in chapter 2.

Feeling into all the experiences you've had that got you in touch with enjoyment and satisfaction is a great way to open and expand your emotional layer.

THE MENTAL LAYER

LAYER: Third

CHAKRA: Solar Plexus

COLOR: Yellow

SIZE: 3 to 8 inches from the body

The mental layer, the third layer of the aura, is connected to the solar plexus chakra and extends about three to eight inches from the body. It vibrates at the frequency of thoughts, belief systems, ego, and sense of self. This layer sits on top of the emotional layer and is higher in frequency.

This layer is where our lower gut instincts are located. It is the place where we decide to be fully committed in our conscious mind to a goal or creative process. It is the location of discernment, as well as where you bring emotions and experiences into concepts and make judgments about the world around you. This is a structured layer, like a communication highway bringing self-consciousness to our soul's experience of creation.

Overdevelopment of this layer can squish the layers above and below it. This leaves less space for the heart and the emotions to exist. People who identify primarily with reason often have a larger mental layer in the field.

While you are doing activities that engage your reason and mental activity, like reading and writing, you are opening and expanding your mental layer. Be mindful and stay curious to what this feels like in your body.

THE ASTRAL LAYER

LAYER: Fourth

CHAKRA: Heart

COLOR: Pink

SIZE: 6 to 12 inches from the body

The astral layer is the fourth layer of the aura and extends six to twelve inches from the body. It overlays the mental layer and is one step higher in frequency. The astral frequency is love. It includes relational love, self-love, and receiving and giving love.

The astral layer is seen as the bridge between spirit and Earth. Like a powerful web, it holds and transforms denser energies into higher frequencies (and vice versa) to allow for communication between the physical and spiritual realms.

When we connect to and expand this layer of the aura, we are giving ourselves a powerful healing. This is often the frequency healers and shamans connect to when giving a healing. The astral layer is the experience of relational love as a continuous circuit of receiving and giving just by being who we are. People with a healthy astral layer are drawn to community and feel comfortable with the give-and-take in relationships.

Those with an underdeveloped aural layer are working toward unconditional and altruistic love, balance in relationship with self-love, and love in relationship with others.

Bringing yourself into a memory or experience of relational love allows you to open and expand the astral layer of your aura. This often causes a feeling of lightness and warmth in the upper chest.

THE ETHERIC TEMPLATE LAYER

LAYER: Fifth

CHAKRA: Throat

COLOR: Cobalt Blue

SIZE: 1.5 to 2 feet from the body

The etheric template is the fifth layer of the auric field and is associated with the throat chakra. It can extend one and a half to two feet from the body, and it is one layer above and a frequency higher than the astral layer. This frequency is associated with communication and self-expression of your personal truth, as well as your ability to receive guidance.

The etheric template layer is the divine map of the lower etheric layer of the aura. Within this layer is all the information of the soul wanting to be made manifest in the physical. Some healers and mystics call it the "body double" or "etheric twin." It is a place of nonjudgment, a place of pure potentiality. The etheric template layer is the architectural plan that supports the creation of the etheric layer and physical body.

This is where you experience yourself as a single instrument that is part of a larger orchestra. What instrument are you? What is the part you choose to play? Open and trust your body to allow the music of the universe to move through you.

> *Notice how it feels in your body when synchronicities or "coincidences" are happening in your life. This is a sign that your etheric template layer is open and expanded. There is a synergy or a high often associated with this experience.*

THE CELESTIAL LAYER

LAYER: Sixth

CHAKRA: Third-Eye

COLOR: Opalescent Pastel Chakra Colors

SIZE: 2 to 2.75 feet from the body

The celestial layer is the sixth layer of the aura. It is created by and fills up with energy from the third-eye chakra, and it extends out about two to two and three-quarters feet from the body. It is one layer above and a frequency higher than the etheric template layer. It is the frequency of creative thinking and ideas, spiritual bliss, unconditional love, and the ecstatic state of oneness many feel during heightened spiritual experiences.

I call it the "bliss layer" because it is the emotional experience and physical sensations of your connection to the spiritual or divine. The colors on this layer look like a shimmery pastel rainbow. It is the layer where we can experience unconditional love, bliss, and spiritual consciousness. Grace and peace are two core qualities of this layer.

People with a strong celestial layer are able to see the larger picture and connect the dots. They love inventing new things or making things better in new and useful ways. They are the visionaries of our world. Sometimes people with a strong celestial layer see the ideas clearly but are not able to implement them because the lower layers of their aura are not as balanced.

Feel into and reflect on your most elevated spiritual moments. These are moments when the celestial layer of your aura is most expanded and open.

THE KETHERIC TEMPLATE LAYER

LAYER: Seventh

CHAKRA: Crown

COLOR: Gold

SIZE: 2.5 to 3.5 feet from the body

The ketheric template layer is the seventh layer of the auric field and is connected to the crown chakra. (The word *keter* means "crown.") It is one layer above and a higher frequency than the celestial layer and extends two and a half to three and a half feet from the body. This is the frequency connected to divine mind and universal consciousness. This layer contains the information of our souls. I work with the angels and archangels on this frequency. They often use gold light, or what I like to call "golden goo," to help seal and repair holes in the aura or repair damaged chakras.

This layer has the larger picture of your life and has the wisdom of who you are on a soul level in the past, present, and future.

People who are rebellious and have issues with authority may find it more challenging to connect with and listen to their higher self-authority.

It can take time to trust that the higher wisdom of who we are has a map of where we are going. Once this trust is established, the ego/mind can relax and have fun with the delivery and experience of how it plays out for them.

When entering your ketheric template layer, you will feel an elevated sense of knowing. This voice always speaks from a place of unity that calms your nervous system. If you are perceiving guidance that causes you to contract or is fear-based, the information is not coming from this layer of your aura.

Conclusion

We have navigated what the aura is, its structure, and its seven main layers. The beautifully complex nature of the aura and its seven layers gives us the capacity to interact with and enjoy experiences in our physical body, feel emotions, use rational thinking, connect relationally, communicate authentically, and elevate to spiritual layers of our being. Understanding the nuances of your aura layers allows you to recognize them in yourself, develop a deeper relationship with your strengths, and pinpoint areas of imbalance for greater healing. We will now move on to the colors of emotions and healing frequencies you can use to cleanse and heal your aura in chapter 2.

CHAPTER TWO

THE COLORS OF THE AURA

O ur aura is like a living, breathing expression of our human experience. Like your personality, every color of the aura can burst forth, billow, or dance, moment to moment, depending on what you are feeling or thinking.

In this chapter we will dive into the frequencies of color and their significance. There are colors connected to emotions, thoughts, healing frequencies, and auric layers. This chapter will be useful for you to refer to as you begin learning to do aura readings for yourself and others in chapter 4.

The Main Colors of the Aura

You can imagine the aura as a color-coded treasure map filled with information and gifts about yourself. Every emotion you feel, mood you experience, thought you have, and mental image you create forms patterns and waves of color and energy throughout your aura. This map also shows where in the aura you will find health and balance or imbalance and struggle. Much of the information you need for healing and cleansing the aura is coded in the various colors. This chapter will help you decipher the colors and give deeper meaning to perceiving the subtle energy around you.

While there is a specific color frequency for each aura layer and chakra, we are all unique with different shades, hues, and tones, so keep in mind that there can be some differentiation between people. Essentially, the more vibrant the colors are in the aura, the more health and well-being are experienced. Vibrant colors are a strong indicator that you have balance in the part of your body in which you are noticing them. If the color is washed-out or lighter than normal, this can indicate an area you don't spend as much time with or where your energy might be depleted.

It's often helpful to give self-care and support to these areas of your life. If the color is darker or muddied, this is usually a sign that there is repressed or blocked emotions or energy. You will want to bring more awareness to these areas and learn exercises or techniques to comfortably release what you have been holding on to.

As you become more adept at reading the colors in your aura and in others' auras, there is a deeper knowledge that, underneath it all, we all want the same things: to be loved, valued, heard, and understood. Most pain and suffering come from the experiences of not having these authentic needs met.

Now let's explore our relationship to color in the aura, as well as what it tells us about our health and well-being and how it relates to ourselves and the world around us.

One versus Many

Due to the family environment, culture, and society we grow up in, we learn to favor some chakras and colors more than others. Our auras take on the colors of our experiences and states of being that we most often feel. The colors you like to wear or have an affinity for often correlate with colors predominantly expressed in your aura.

For example, open-hearted people who enjoy being around others can have large amounts of rose pink in their aura, healers have many shades of pink, purple, and green around them, and there is yellow in the auras of people who tend to be in their heads and have constant mental activity.

Questions: What colors bring you a sense of peace? What colors do you like to wear or decorate your living space with? What colors do you tend to avoid? Ask your friends and family members as well. Are their answers different? Do the colors they like line up with what you sense in them? What colors do they associate with you and your personality?

RED

ASSOCIATION: Root Chakra

PERSONALITY TRAITS: Solidity, Stability, Embodiment

BALANCED QUALITIES: Vitality, Grounded, Security

IMBALANCED QUALITIES: Fear, Poor Health, Low Energy

The color red represents primal life force, safety, and strong connection to the Earth. It is the color of a healthy root chakra. Red is the primary and densest frequency in the aura. People with a lot of ruby red in their fields have strong physical energy and vitality. This is why athletes have a lot of red in their auras.

Lighter shades of rose red or pink red are often created with feelings of love or being amorous.

If you are experiencing lighter shades of red when feeling into your root chakra or the lower parts of your body, this can be a sign that your energy is depleted. There may also be a leak or tear in your field.

Darker colors mixed with red indicate a block or a trapped energy in that area of the aura. For example, I often see red-brown in the lower part of the aura around the hips when clients are suppressing their emotions. Suppressed anger causes a sticky, dense, muddy-red color to appear in the aura. Red with black can indicate that the block has been hanging around for a while, and multiple layers of clearing might be needed over time.

I perceive physical inflammation in the body as pink to dark red depending on the intensity of pain. It looks like ribbons of energy that cling close to the physical body.

Shame can look like rusty red or even a healthy red, but it has a prickly feel to it—almost like the feeling of high winds blowing sand in your face at the beach. I've often seen shame rise or seep out of clients' bones as they process early experiences.

ORANGE

ASSOCIATION: Sacral Chakra

PERSONALITY TRAITS: Vibrancy, Boldness, Magnetism

BALANCED QUALITIES: Adventurousness, Charisma, Creativeness

IMBALANCED QUALITIES: Deceptiveness, Addiction, Depression

Bright, vibrant orange is the color of a healthy sacral chakra and is associated with joy, healthy pride, playfulness, pleasure, and creativity. I love seeing people with this color in their fields because it means they have a zest for life. They are able to feel a myriad of textures and qualities in the foods they eat and in the people around them. They are able to tune into their emotions and how they feel about things with ease. They are adept at reading the ambience of their environment and can have powerful charisma and be very charming. Sensual people tend to express a lot of orange within their field.

People with orange in their auras love to feel the pleasures in life, but too much can lead to imbalanced qualities if it is not balanced with the physical, mental, and spiritual layers of the aura. The inability to feel personal satisfaction and joy can lead to depression. This can appear in shades of white-orange or muddied orange near the pelvis.

Varying shades of orange-red with pink appear in the aura when a person feels deep satisfaction, exuberant joy, tenderness, or grounded excitement.

Tenderness is a beautiful mix of orange and rose pink that creates shades of coral in the aura, depending on how much the emotional and astral layers are open and relating. The rose-orange colors of passion are exhilarating to see and experience.

YELLOW

ASSOCIATIONS: Solar Plexus Chakra and Mental Layer

PERSONALITY TRAITS: Discernment, Intelligence, Clarity

BALANCED QUALITIES: Courageousness, Centeredness, Freedom

IMBALANCED QUALITIES: Fixedness, Emptiness, Anxiety

Bright yellow is the color of a healthy solar plexus chakra and the mental layer of the aura. It is present in people who have a strong clarity of who they are and what they want. It is the color of intelligence, reason, and communication of thoughts and belief systems.

People with yellow in their auras feel confident to express their ideas and belief systems—sometimes so much that they don't realize others aren't interested or aren't listening anymore! They also have a strong connection to personal responsibility and self-discipline. They can be dedicated to what is right and to balancing things that are in service to themselves and the world around them.

Because the mental layer of the aura is yellow, many thoughts appear yellow. If you are someone who uses reason to negotiate the world around you or to relate to others, you most likely have yellow in your aura.

When people are feeling guilty about something or are in denial, I see strong flashes of yellow burst forth from the center of their solar plexus chakra. Perfectionism and obsessive-compulsive disorder (OCD) are more amber-yellow and have a texture of rigidity, like something being pulled taught. Yellow blended with different shades of pink, like peach, is the color of healthy self-worth and self-esteem.

GREEN

ASSOCIATION: Heart Chakra

PERSONALITY TRAITS: Compassion, Healing, Generosity

BALANCED QUALITIES: Lovingness, Empathy, Gentleness

IMBALANCED QUALITIES: Self-Sacrifice, Despair, Loneliness

People with a lot of green in their field understand the interconnectedness of humanity and nature and the importance of community. They like to work as part of a team, and it is easy for them to trust and get along with others. They are musically inclined and are connected to the relational field of the arts. They are gentle, have empathy for others, and genuinely care about others. If you have ever been told you're easy to talk to or are a great listener, you probably have some green in your field.

People with green in their field hold great space for others, sometimes to their own detriment. Putting others' needs first and neglecting their own can lead to jealousy, which looks like a muddied green. Envy is an even darker green in the field. Sometimes it is such a dark green that it looks almost black. These frequencies are very unhealthy for the heart and the auric field and can spread from the heart and upper chest area to the rest of the field. These colors repel people.

I have seen exquisite emerald green in the auras of people who are healers. These people have incredible compassion and the core quality of acceptance in their field, which puts others at ease.

BLUE

ASSOCIATIONS: Throat Chakra, Etheric Layer, Etheric Template Layer

PERSONALITY TRAITS: Strong Communication, Trustworthiness, Resourcefulness

BALANCED QUALITIES: Honesty, Receptiveness, Open-Mindedness

IMBALANCED QUALITIES: Dishonesty, Dismissiveness, Hyperactivity

People with blue in their field are perceptive and have great timing. They highly value honesty and being true to their word. They are open to receiving and communicating their divine truth and may also have the gift of clairaudience, the ability to receive and translate information from higher beings, guides, and angels. Adept understanding of divination is also a blue trait.

Sky blue is present in the aura of people who are skillful with concepts and designs. These people are cleverly inventive and resourceful and have the ability to synthesize the information around them and communicate it in a way that inspires and connects with others. Poets, writers, orators, and architects tend to have this color.

Blue is the frequency of being connected to living in your divine truth and purpose. Learning to know, trust, and value your truth is the key to creating vibrant sky blue in your aura. Your truth is not the same as another's. For example, if you are telling others what they want to hear instead of standing in your own unique perspective, such as not asking your boss for that raise you know you deserve, you are not in touch with your truth. This causes the blue in your throat chakra or aura to be either too dark or washed-out.

INDIGO

ASSOCIATION: Third-Eye Chakra

PERSONALITY TRAITS: Visionary, Creator, Mystic

BALANCED QUALITIES: Spirituality, Creativity, Problem-Solving

IMBALANCED QUALITIES: Hypervigilance, Arrogance, Aloofness

Indigo is the color of the third-eye chakra. This color is associated with royalty, majesty, grace, and access to the spiritual or higher realms.

To be enveloped in indigo feels like dropping into the abyss of the cosmos and being hugged by a warm blanket. It is the vibration of divine love, unconditional love, and bliss.

People with indigo in their field are adept at creatively solving complex problems. They are agile with larger concepts because they can see the bigger picture. They often get much insight from their dreams and tend to be visionaries, psychics, mediums, and clairvoyants.

Excess indigo around the head can mean the person is ungrounded and hypervigilant. Some people perceive them as inauthentic or aloof if they are disconnected from the lower part of their body. I often see thyroid problems in psychics if they are disconnected from their heart and feel separate from others. Lacking the rose pink of the astral layer to buffer the high energy, they run through their body putting tremendous strain on the thyroid.

Many people claim to see purple near people's heads instead of indigo. This is usually because they are seeing a mix of rose and indigo, which is the color of unconditional love. Lavender is a higher, more refined frequency, in the purple family, that is used to stimulate the immune system and help kill infections and viruses.

GOLD

ASSOCIATIONS: Crown Chakra and Ketheric Template Layer

PERSONALITY TRAITS: Angelic, Oracle, Sage

BALANCED QUALITIES: Global Consciousness, Direct Knowing, Wisdom

IMBALANCED QUALITIES: Impersonalism, Disconnectedness, Porousness

Gold is the color of the ketheric template layer of the auric field and has a very high frequency—the frequency of alchemy, which is one of the most powerful to heal your aura with because it instantly connects you with the angelic realm.

When people have gold in their aura, it means they are a mature soul and have developed a strong connection to higher consciousness. They have done the work to let go of their ego's need to be right and can surrender to the divine plan. They are much more interested in doing what is best for humanity. They are typically being taken care of by the angels and have a divine mission or purpose for being on Earth.

Gold is also the color of Kundalini energy. Kundalini is the unitive relationship between the divine and the soul interwoven through every chakra and around the body. The relationship with Kundalini develops slowly over time as the person and their auric field become cleaner, stronger, and more integrated in every layer of their aura.

Gold is also the color of your soul's essence. When the golden soul essence in every cell of the body is activated and expanded, it looks like reflecting sparkles everywhere in the aura. The first time I witnessed it in my aura, I gasped in astonishment and felt ecstatic bliss. I felt like I was home.

WHITE

ASSOCIATIONS: Light Body, Crown Chakra

PERSONALITY TRAITS: Purity, Innocence, Sage

BALANCED QUALITIES: Etherealness, Wisdom, Integration

IMBALANCED QUALITIES: Porousness, Airiness, Spiritual Bypassing

Pure white is the frequency of the higher angelic realms, purity, and innocence. It is the color of the light body, which is a higher vibration and layer of the aura than the lower seven layers. It is also associated with the crown chakra on the emotional layer of the aura.

White possesses a quality of pure honesty disconnected from ego and outcome. It looks and feels like fluffy, billowy clouds or sometimes a pure white fog that envelops the body. Sometimes people can see a white fog or shroud that surrounds everything when they have had a spiritual experience or after deep meditation. This is a sign they opened up to a non-dual experience, which is a state of consciousness where everything is connected in perfect balance.

White is generally the color of peace or peacefulness, but seeing white in the field can also have a very different meaning. Fear appears white with jagged, sharp edges. To know the difference, you will need to use your feelings and not rely just on vision. Fear has a frozen quality to it when it stays in the auric field for long periods of time. Initially it can feel prickly, electric, or frenetic when someone is in an active state of fear.

The Minor Colors of the Aura

In addition to the seven main colors, the aura contains many other colors that may appear less often. Each color emits a unique frequency and represents different qualities. The following are just a few of the minor colors.

ROSE

Rose is the color of the fourth auric layer of the field, the astral layer. The frequency of rose is one of the most powerful healing tools we possess, and we have access to this through the heart chakra and our experiences of love in relationship to others. This could be any relational experience with plants, animals, people, and even places. It could be the love of your first pet, a heart-opening experience watching the sunset, or a moment you experienced in nature when your heart leapt as a result of the beauty around you. It also can come through the loving relationships of your friends, partners, and family.

Rose is the color of love and nurturing. It is the color of the mother archetype. I have seen many mothers holding their infants with auras full of rose light. Their heart chakras blossom wide open in the expression of love for their newborn child. Pink is the color of loving kindness and acceptance as well as young, blossoming love.

Compassion can have red shades combined with pink, creating a beautiful coral color. Gratitude is rose mixed with gold light. It is a frequency of master healing and transmutation. This means it can change dark colors or stuck emotions in your aura to a more positive version closer to your soul's divine truth.

Holding deep gratitude for others opens and heals not only your aura but also theirs. Loving the places in yourself that are in pain and not pushing them away allows profound healing to occur. Having gratitude for the embodied lessons that come from your pain is one of the most potent ways you can heal yourself.

BLACK

The color black can mean many different things in the field, so it is important to tap into your own experience of spaciousness or compaction within your body as you perceive the frequency of black. I try not to assign judgment right away when I see colors like black in the field. If black is there and having a negative impact on my client, then judgment from me will cause it to compact even more. I have to become different frequencies, like rose pink (compassion), orange (joy), and gold (essence), to create space in the aura for the compaction to clear.

Black is most often repressed emotions that have been hanging out in the aura for a long time. Most emotions we perceive as painful if held in long enough will turn from light gray to dark gray and then black. They are nothing to fear and just need a lot of love to clear.

Hate is the only emotion I've seen as originally black in color. It's like a thick ink that poisons the auric field and trickles down into the physical body over time. Resentment cripples the heart chakra and astral layer of the field. It starts out dark red and over time turns black with a jagged red outline.

Black is also the color of one of the most powerful forces of manifestation. It is often referred to as the majestic void or the primal womb of creation. Meditating within this space is one of the most powerful learning experiences I've had. To sit in raw potentiality before it moves into the sphere of creation and then manifestation was very humbling to my ego. After this, I knew I could never claim my creations as my own but as co-creations with the divine. How to source and create from the primal womb of creation is a masterful way of manifestation that I now teach in my "Manifest Like a Master" classes.

VIOLET

Violet is another master healing frequency that transmutes negative energies, stagnant energies, and dark clouds from the aura. It also transmutes karma. I don't see this color in people's auras except during healings when the energy of this frequency comes in the form of grace when they need it.

I wasn't aware of the power of the violet frequency until about three years into my private practice. While working with a new client, I noticed a dense collection of dark gray clouds in her upper chest and heart area. I spent some time on the lower layers of the aura, clearing and restructuring the channels of energy. Within a few minutes all of the dense energy evaporated into thin air. I was astounded. She took a deep breath in and said she felt like a heavy weight had been lifted off her. She came in a few weeks later and emphatically exclaimed, "Laura, I feel like a new person. I thought I was experiencing love before, but now I really feel what love is!"

I later learned there is much information about the violet flame. It is also referred to as "the flame of forgiveness" or "the mercy flame." It is often attributed to St. Germain, an ascended master. I find that the flame comes when it is needed and not for everyone all the time.

SILVER

Silver is another high frequency of light that is used to help kill infection and clean areas of the aura after removing debris in the astral layer. It is super conductive and takes a lot of energy and coherency to use during healings. Sometimes the crown chakra has a more white-silver or gold-silver hue to it.

I see silver in my client's aura and higher aura layers when they are actively working on their soul's life plan, mission, and purpose. Silver strengthens the nervous system over time to receive more refined communication with the higher realms.

Gray is typically the color of unexpressed and repressed emotions like sadness and grief. Other emotions that appear gray in the field are despair, apathy, helplessness, and hopelessness.

Collections of gray colors, or clouds, in the aura can point to physical health issues if they have been there for a while. If you clear them and they repeatedly come back, there may be something in the area you need to take a look at.

Certain medications for depression and the thyroid and sometimes birth control can mute the colors of the chakras. Estrogen-repressing pills cause a shroud of gray over the entire field and shut down the sacral chakra, making everything gray. I have worked with breast cancer survivors to help clear the gray built-up energy in their auras and keep their sacral chakras healthy while they are required to be on this type of medication.*

This information is simply something to consider—you should continue to take any medications prescribed to you by a medical professional.

RAINBOW

When people have a very healthy aura, all the rainbow colors of the aura layers and main chakras are vibrant and symmetrical in size. This is a sign of emotional maturity and healthy integration of the body, mind, and spirit throughout all the layers of the aura.

It is a sign that they don't hang on to personal judgments or grudges and no longer identify with the inner bully. They have a deeper sense of safety and trust in the universe and that everything is transpiring for their highest good, even if it doesn't feel like it in the moment.

The celestial layer of the aura has pastel rainbow colors that look shimmery as they move. It is more refined in frequency than the vibrant rainbow colors seen in the emotional layer.

DIM OR BRIGHT COLORS

In general, the more vibrant the colors in the aura are, the more health and well-being are experienced in that area of the body. The darker or more washed-out the colors are in a certain area, the weaker or more blocked the energy is. The colors you have an aversion to can also indicate the aura layers or chakras you have a weaker connection with or the parts of yourself you have yet to fully embrace.

The colors of the aura are of such a pure and vibrant saturation and quality that I rarely get to see in the physical world. Experiencing them is a joy I never tire of. I feel it's an honor to explore the swirling cosmos within ourselves and others.

Conclusion

Becoming adept at reading the colors in the auric field made me more comfortable with myself and others. It is helpful to use a nonjudgmental space of exploration as you feel into the colors of your aura. This will allow you to experience more of the information stored in the textures and shades of your energy and emotions while creating space for them to move out of your aura. In the next chapter we will look at the chakras in your aura that help you take in and move energy, as well as the many forms of energy healing that support the structure of your aura and physical health.

CHAPTER THREE

AURAS AND ENERGY HEALING

You were born with a self-healing ability, and through the use of various energy healing methods, it can be awakened within you.

In this chapter we will explore the broader field of energy healing to give you a greater understanding of how your aura is powered through the function of your chakras. You will learn about a few of the most common methods that energy healers and energy practitioners use to bring the aura back into balance. We will delve into details about each of the seven chakras.

This will give you a basic foundation and understanding of your chakras and valuable ways to support your energy before we move into aura healing in chapter 5.

Energy Healing

Energy healing is the practice of accessing energy from within and around the body and channeling it to bring greater healing and balance to ourselves or others.

This life force energy has many names from different cultures and traditions. In China it's called *chi* (*qi*). There is extensive charting and mapping of the movement of chi through energy channels that dates back many centuries. This knowledge is used today in Traditional Chinese Medicine, most commonly known as acupuncture. In Japan this energy is called *ki*, and it is from this word that Reiki was formed. In India they call this life force energy *prana*. Yoga is a form of breathing and movement techniques used to harness prana from the universal energy field around us and strengthen the prana within the body. In the early 1900s Dr. Wilhelm Reich, one of the early influencers of modern energy healing, "rediscovered" the same energy and called it "orgone energy."

There are four main elements we receive this vital energy from:

Air: We take in prana with every breath, and it circulates through our body to nourish us. We also take in prana and universal energy all around us through the pores in our skin. Our chakra centers are designed to receive and transmit energy. As they spin, they receive and give energy with each revolution, just like our bodies receive oxygen with every inhale and exhale of carbon dioxide.

Earth: We take in energy from the Earth through the soles of our feet and our root chakra. When our root and sacral chakras are strong and healthy, we naturally absorb the pulsations of the red frequency that supports the physical body and solidifies the auric field. This is why we often use the phrase "being grounded." It is a reference to feeling solid in our aura and physical body because of our strong connection to the Earth's energy.

Sun: We absorb the energy of sunlight through our eyes and skin. This energy strengthens our immune system, lifts our mood, and increases well-being. Sunbathing before 11 a.m. or after 3 p.m. for 20 minutes or less is recommended to absorb and replenish chi. Taking in too much sunlight can also drain our chi.

Water: Water is essential for life. Water also holds the imprints of energy, which is why it is a sacred symbol and is often used in rituals and healing methods to anchor and support a specific transmission that is desired. Water is also cleansing, washing away impurities in the body and the aura.

AYURVEDA

Ayurveda is one of the oldest forms of energy healing. It pulls from the ancient teachings and information of the Hindu Vedas. Ayurvedic philosophy explains how the five elements of air, space, fire, water, and earth come together into three harmonious pairs called the *doshas*: *vata*, *pitta*, and *kapha*.

Individuals often have a mixture of more than one dosha. Stress, seasonal changes, lifestyle, diet, sleep, thoughts, travel, and weather can all create interference with our doshas. Ayurveda is a preventive and healing system of using foods, herbs, specific exercises, meditations, and breathing techniques to support these balances. It teaches us how to live in harmony with our doshic makeup.

Ayurveda uses multiple approaches, allowing it to affect multiple aura layers for more balance and well-being. One of these approaches is the branch of Vedic knowledge called yoga.

YOGA

Yoga has numerous approaches and disciplines for accessing and harnessing external and internal prana for physical and spiritual uses. Some of these are breathwork, meditation, devotional singing and chanting, and physical movements synchronized with the breath.

These techniques distribute and promote the flow of prana throughout the body.

Yoga classes typically start with a short prayer. They then move on to breathing exercises followed by yoga poses called *asanas* and end with time for inner meditation and relaxation. Working with an instructor initially will help you learn the exercises and what it feels like to drop into subtle energy in your body.

Nowadays it is usually easy to find a yoga studio nearby with classes to support your particular dosha and needs. Yoga is an excellent tool for bringing structure and balance to the aura. It is one of several select practices mentioned in this book for maintaining and strengthening aura health over time.

REIKI

Reiki was formed as a healing spiritual practice by Japanese Buddhist Mikao Usui in 1922. *Rei* means "soul or divine wisdom," and *ki* means "vital energy." Reiki practitioners are trained to receive and connect to the energy from ancient healing symbols that hold universal energy and consciousness. They pass on this universal consciousness by staying in a state of receiving and allowing the other person to take in whatever energy their system is comfortable receiving. Reiki can simultaneously affect all the aura layers, giving the receiver an experience of relaxation and space for many layers of the aura to unwind. For example, emotional stress, anxiety, and physical ailments are sometimes caused by the aura layers being bound too tightly by the mind. Reiki healings relax the aura as a whole and can bring great symmetry to the entire auric field. It is a great personal practice for self-healing and aura cleansing. Reiki can be done remotely or in-person with light touch on the body, typically with both hands on the shoulders.

TRADITIONAL CHINESE MEDICINE
Traditional Chinese Medicine (TCM) is a system of energy healing developed in China thousands of years ago and is still used today as a primary source of health care for one-quarter of the world's population. The most common concept of balance and harmony—the yin-yang symbol—comes from TCM. It describes the interdependent relationship between opposing yet complementary forces. TCM works differently than Western medicine. It is a preventive form of healing that looks at the entire body as many parts that are balancing a whole. If one part gets pulled in a certain direction, it affects all the other parts. Balance is restored by supporting all the pieces so they can come back into relationship again. These pieces are represented in TCM as the five elements: wood, fire, earth, metal, and water.

TCM practitioners can locate where imbalances are in your body, mind, emotions, and spirit. They have different methods to strengthen organ function and support good health, including acupuncture, herbs and herbal formulas, cupping, moxibustion, *gua sha*, and massage.

ACUPUNCTURE

Acupuncture is one of the most widely known forms of TCM. It is the art of working with the energy channels in the body called meridians. Energy meridians look like streams of energy running through the physical body and first layer of the aura, the etheric field. There are thousands of tiny points along these meridians that look like little funnels, which are called the minor chakras. Acupuncturists press small needles in the skin to pierce the center of the chakras and spin them to encourage movement of energy through the meridians. These treatments can help balance hormones, lower inflammation, and restore health in vital organs, giving you more energy and helping prevent chronic illness.

Acupuncturists have some of the longest, most in-depth training in the world of energy healing. It is one of only a few forms of energy healing that has been somewhat accepted by Western medical science, and licensed practitioners are currently able to accept insurance in some parts of the United States and other parts of the world.

QIGONG

Qigong is an ancient method of moving chi, or qi, through the body and energy meridians using breath and synchronized movements of the hands, feet, and body. The practices remove blocked chi, increase its free flow, and distribute it evenly throughout the aura. It is an excellent method of personal self-energy healing for clearing and cleansing the energy and aura. People are typically taught in group classes, which allows the teacher to transmit the experience of subtle energy to the students.

A typical session of Qigong involves a series of continued breathing and moving exercises to open a specific channel, about five minutes. Then you'll switch to another channel until you have moved through all the major channels and achieved symmetry and balance in the aura. I have seen Qigong students expand the circumference of their field three times the size by the end of a session. This technique is one of the fastest ways I know to open and unblock energy channels and make your aura bright and vibrant again. It also increases the amount of energy you can hold in your aura over time, making you energetically strong and resilient. It is a powerful way to open and balance all your chakras and aura layers together.

CHAKRA HEALING

The knowledge of chakras and healing for self-realization has been handed down over many centuries throughout India, Tibet, and other parts of Asia.

All of the methods of energy healing mentioned in this chapter benefit the chakras in one form or another. Your ability to bring your awareness to these powerful centers of energy gives you entry into different aspects of yourself. Chakras are like doorways opening you to all seven layers of the human aura. They give you the ability to unlock your potential and to experience the essence of who you are. When you slow down and attune to the specific frequency of a chakra, you have access to experiencing it in your aura layer. This is how the chakras and layers of the aura allow you to perceive and interact with the world around you. This takes a lot of awareness, intention, compassion, and joy, which is why chakra meditations are so powerful.

Specific chakra healing and restructuring is very specialized work. The healer must know how to hold different frequencies of energy with intention for long periods of time, when and how to restructure all seven layers of the aura within each chakra, and how to find the precise placement of the chakra in relationship to the person's physical body, organs, and other chakras and aura layers. The work is precise, and I highly recommend you only work with healers who have had extensive training and experience in this area.

The Chakras

You happen to have thousands of tiny chakras all over your body. These are where acupuncturists put thin needles in people's skin to open and direct energy flow. There are seven locations where the energy meridians cross multiple times, which is where the seven major chakras are located. You can think of them like central train station hubs. All the minor and major energy meridians connect at these seven central points to exchange and distribute energy. They are located in the physical body at the tailbone, the sacrum, the solar plexus, the heart, the throat, the spot between the eyebrows, and the very top of the head.

The chakras look like spinning wheels with intake valves that absorb energy from the universal energy field around you. They split and syphon the energy into seven specific frequencies. These are the rainbow colors you often see depicted with the chakras. Each frequency is a color of the light spectrum and corresponds to the aura layers (see chapter 1). Every organ in the body primarily digests one of these color frequencies. That digested energy is then carried out by the meridians to where it is needed throughout the body.

ROOT CHAKRA

The root chakra is the funnel of energy that is located at the perineum, in front of the tailbone. It moves vertically up into the pelvis and connects into the center of the sacral chakra. There is a joint relationship between the two chakras from which the creation of our life force and vitality arise. This is why it is sometimes difficult to separate some of the qualities of the root and sacral chakra—they both directly support each other.

Balanced Attributes: People with a balanced root chakra have strong physical health, vitality, and a solid connection to their body. They feel safe and secure and have stability in their lives. They tend to be adventurous and have a strong presence.

Imbalanced Attributes: The biggest issue with excess energy in the root chakra is repressed life force. This causes a tremendous amount of compacted energy to be stuck in the upper thighs. This blocks those people from feeling the freedom of connection to their personal power. They may still have a strong presence, but they lack vibrancy and have a sense of being weighed down in life. They often complain of feeling heavy, even if they are not overweight.

With a lack of life force and vitality, people with an underdeveloped root chakra are more susceptible to illness. They tend to be prone to systemic inflammation, joint issues, and autoimmune diseases. The entire aura tends to look porous or feel airy. They may rely on those around them to be their grounding and will feel more energized around people with a strong root chakra.

SACRAL CHAKRA

The sacral chakra is located two to four inches below the belly button, depending on the length of the person's torso. It is vibrant orange like carrot juice and shares its center with the root chakra. It is the chakra that takes in and metabolizes the frequency of emotions and creates the emotional layer of the aura. It is also the location of our life force and passion for life.

Balanced Attributes: A balanced sacral chakra gives us the capacity to feel deserving of pleasure and to enjoy it while taking up space. Many say it is connected to our sexuality and sensuality. It regulates the amount of energy and comfort in our personal power that we allow ourselves to have at any given time and is balanced with our ability to personally enjoy the textures and qualities of things around us.

Imbalanced Attributes: Overdevelopment of this chakra without balance can cause a person to be overly aggressive or jump to anger quickly. They may be emotionally volatile and unable to self-soothe or not able to see another person's reality outside their own.

Fear of being big is one of the most common complaints I hear from my clients when their sacral chakra is underbalanced. They were often made to feel like they or their needs were too much when they were younger. They may experience stage fright or fear of speaking in front of groups. They tend to give their power away by squeezing the back of the sacral chakra, which slows down the chakra's ability to take in energy. This causes their aura to shrink in size. They do this to be loved by others and to be accepted as part of a group.

SOLAR PLEXUS CHAKRA

The solar plexus chakra is located above the belly button, half an inch to one inch below the opening of the rib cage. This chakra is vibrant lemon yellow and creates the mental layer of the aura.

Balanced Attributes: People with a strong solar plexus have a powerful sense of self. With their quick, sharp mind, they are able to balance gut instinct with reason. They know what they want, and they know how to get it.

Imbalanced Attributes: When this chakra is out of balance, the person sees situations as only black or white with no alternatives. Overdevelopment of this layer can squish out the layers above and below it, which leaves less space for the heart and the emotions. People who believe that emotions are not safe or who identify primarily with reason often have a larger mental layer.

When people are disconnected from their solar plexus chakra, they tend to be swayed easily by others' opinions and find it difficult to decide what they want in life. They have a hard time digesting what's happening to them emotionally or physically and may rely on others to make decisions for them.

HEART CHAKRA

The heart chakra is located at the center of the chest next to the heart and on the breastbone. Its color is emerald green.

Balanced Attributes: People with a balanced heart chakra are drawn to community and feel comfortable giving to and receiving from others. They have a beautiful, compassionate nature and know how to take care of and honor themselves while maintaining loving and strong boundaries. They read others well and have great social timing. They can feel into the needs of others and know the right timing of when to give support and when to step back.

Imbalanced Attributes: Without relational love and support, people with an imbalanced heart chakra are often filled with despair and loneliness. They may feel like others take advantage of them and often take on the role of caretaker or martyr. They feel they need to take care of others to be loved and get their needs met but end up resentful.

We as a society are working toward realizing unconditional and altruistic love. You might find it challenging to feel into your own needs or the needs of others. Some find it confusing to see others connecting in loving ways with close bonds when they have never experienced such care. I have had some clients say they felt like the whole world was faking love and connection until they had their first heart chakra–opening experience.

Balancing the open expression of the heart chakra is one of the greatest challenges I've seen working with clients in the United States. Our society rewards output: giving and doing. Taking and receiving are often done through covert means to get our needs met because socially we don't want to enjoy it "too much" for fear of being considered greedy, selfish, self-centered, or narcissistic.

THROAT CHAKRA

The throat chakra is located in the middle of the throat and connects to the thyroid. It is a bright sky blue.

Balanced Attributes: People with a balanced throat chakra are trustworthy, great listeners, and have a strong receptive quality that allows others to feel seen and heard. Their values and morals cannot be compromised. They don't like to gossip, and they speak their truth from a place of compassion and what is correct for themselves. As part of a larger co-creation, they trust that a higher power has their back, and they connect into divine synchronicity easily. Their openness to higher-level guidance enables them to discern patterns and connections where others see chaos.

Imbalanced Attributes: People with a blocked throat chakra are disconnected from their life purpose and mission. They feel undervalued as well as undeserving and have a hard time asking for what they want, or they make do with what they have and try to get their needs met through sources that are not aligned with their values. They can be excellent storytellers, poets, and speakers with others' concepts but may lack their own ideas.

THIRD-EYE CHAKRA

The third-eye chakra is located in the center of the head, level with or just above the eyebrows. It shares its center with the crown chakra. The color of this chakra is perceived as anywhere from purple to indigo.

Balanced Attributes: When this chakra is in balance, people experience sharp creative thinking, the ability to see the larger picture, and a greater vision of where they are headed in life. They sense a deep satisfaction and certainty in the divine path laid out for them and have faith in a greater purpose and plan. A gift—although sometimes it doesn't always feel like it—is guidance in "knowing" the right step to take.

Imbalanced Attributes: In this chakra, the most common imbalance I see is the overuse of the front of the chakra in the forehead. When the front of the third-eye chakra is too large, it is in fight-or-flight mode. The front of the chakra can expand 10 inches or more and be pulled so far forward that, while sitting at a comfortable social distance from such people, I can feel their third-eye chakra energy hitting me! This leaves the chakra in the back quite blocked, which means the person is typically seeing through a lens of fear of what might be as opposed to what really is.

It takes a balanced third-eye chakra in the front and back to have clear vision, to receive energy and information from a relaxed and receptive state, and to see what is actually there and respond to it with creative intelligence. When the third-eye chakra has a front-to-back balance in symmetry, the nervous system is relaxed and responsive.

CROWN CHAKRA

The crown chakra is the funnel of energy located at the top center of the head. It moves vertically down into the center of the third-eye chakra. Our experience of being connected to oneness, bliss, and divine mind arises from this joint relationship between the two chakras. It is why many psychics, mediums, and healers attribute colors like purple, indigo, white, or gold to these two chakras. They bring the higher experiences of who we are on a soul level down into embodiment.

Balanced Attributes: People with a balanced crown chakra experience synchronicity in all things. They are often called "old souls" because of their sage-like wisdom. Their aura feels bright with a luminous quality around it. They easily access grace, faith, and divine mind. With a refined quality and gentle touch, these people can have a strong connection to the angelic realms.

Imbalanced Attributes: Time management is challenging for people with an unbalanced crown chakra. They live up in universal or angelic time. They tend to swoop in at synchronistic moments only to space out and miss an appointment. People tend to call them airy, flighty, or spacey. Sometimes they expect others to read their minds. When the crown is disconnected from the throat chakra or heart chakra, those people can speak in fanatical terms, creating fear and confusion in others. The crown chakra balances the central nervous system, so issues like migraines, tension headaches, nervousness, and some anxiety disorders may be due to imbalances in the crown.

Conclusion

This chapter has introduced you to a variety of time-tested methods of aura healing, each with a specific and valuable avenue to work with the human aura. Chakra meditations, yoga, and Qigong are excellent ways to explore your subtle energy while strengthening and balancing it. I highly recommend picking one of these methods to support your growth.

Now that you have learned about the specific layers, colors, and chakras in your aura, you can begin to home in on areas you would like to enhance and support. In the following chapters, we will move into feeling and reading the subtle energies, as well as cleansing, strengthening, and maintaining your aura health.

CHAPTER FOUR

READING THE AURA

Reading your aura requires you to slow down and be present with yourself in new areas. In this chapter you will learn how to tap into and feel subtle energy along with multiple exercises and techniques to practice seeing energy. These basic techniques will help open you to being with your aura and understanding its colors. You will use what you learned in the first three chapters to explore and improve your skills.

To See, We Must Feel

As we explore seeing the aura and the colors in the auric field, keep in mind that sensing and feeling are valuable skills that will help you perceive healthy or unhealthy versions of color in your auric field.

I have found that "feeling" a color is often easier and much more useful than "seeing" a color. This is because emotions and thoughts have both a frequency of color and a texture. Different emotions can have the same or similar color but feel very different. For example, purity or innocence is often seen as soft white, while fear is also white but is jagged in appearance and pulsates erratically.

When my guides said they were going to turn off my vision so I could focus on the basics for a while, I went along with it without hesitation. Little did I know it would take years to have my vision back in a healthy way! This forced me to drop into my kinesthetic hands-on perceptions. It also strengthened my ability to feel emotions and thoughts in the auric field. After a short while I was able to identify dozens of emotions and colors in my clients from just the feeling of the frequency.

My vision gradually returned in the same manner it does when you go to the ophthalmologist to get a new pair of glasses. Over time, what looked like a blurry blob of color became more defined until I could see an outline. Then I started to see full pictures and connections and relationships between different layers of the aura. It took years to build up those abilities, but being able to feel the frequency, color, and connecting emotion or thought is far more accurate and useful than seeing alone ever was.

Plus, delivery of information to my clients from a place of empathy and compassion allows them to feel seen and heard. I have observed many psychics over the years see clearly but without an open heart. This can cause fear or a feeling of being judged to arise in the client. We will go more deeply into how to see and experience colors for the purpose of cleansing and healing your aura later in this chapter.

FEELING SUBTLE ENERGY

Subtle energy is a more refined frequency of energy, and even though the particles are moving faster, you have to slow down to be able to connect with it. The more present you are in your body, the greater the chance you have of feeling the subtle energy within and around you. This state is called simply "the state of being." It can be a challenging state for many of us to achieve for any length of time as we are taught that "doing" is how we succeed and get our needs met in life.

You are continuously perceiving subtle energy around you and reacting before your conscious mind can register it. Responding to subtle energy is instinctual because you are made of it and many layers of aura are attuned to it. Have you ever had a gut instinct about someone that turned out to be right? Maybe you've walked into a room and gotten a bad vibe. These are some of the ways you perceive subtle energy through different layers of your aura beyond your conscious thoughts. Learning to trust these sensations, instincts, and vibes as valuable information will assist you in reading your aura and perceiving these subtle energies.

FEELING EXERCISE
Comfortably seated with your palms facing up, sit for a moment and bring your attention to the skin on your palms and see if you can feel the air touching them. As you bring more awareness here, what sensations do you notice? Do you feel

a pulsation, tingling, or warmth? Now briefly rub your hands together to create some friction and feel the energy you are creating. Open the palms of your hands and use the middle finger of the opposite hand to slowly trace the center of the palm, where the minor chakra is located, in a clockwise circle. (Do this for about one minute on each hand.) As you do this, imagine your hand is filling with energy and see if you can feel a small ball of energy forming in the center of your palms. If you can't feel the subtle energy, slow down even more.

ENERGY BALL EXERCISE

Once you have created a small ball of energy in each palm, bring both palms together slowly and see if you can feel the energy balls connecting. Play with the sensations you experience as you slowly push your hands together and farther apart. What do you feel? Do the balls feel bouncy? Do you feel one ball or two? Can you feel the funnels of the minor chakras in your palms spinning and connecting even though your hands are pulled apart? How far can you pull your palms away while they're still facing each other and you're still feeling the energy exchange between the two? Now see if you can start packing and growing your energy ball—like a snowball. How condensed or big can you make it?

FEELING THE BOUNDARY OF YOUR AURA
Having done the subtle energy exploration with your hands, briefly rub your hands together again and feel them light up with subtle energy. Slowly extend your arms to the edge of your aura, which is about an arm's length outward. Imagine what it would feel like if you could trace the subtle energy boundary of your aura. What does your aura bubble feel like? Is it porous or solid? Structured or fluid? Is there symmetry in your aura boundary? What side do you feel more attracted to? Is there more energy in your head or your legs? Moving very slowly, what colors do you feel or see easily in your mind's eye?

Seeing the Aura

Did you know most people don't actually see subtle energy with their physical eyes? Even well-known psychics and healers who track subtle energy accurately do so from the part of the brain that uses imagery. They call this the "mind screen." Many people have success by picking up the subtle energy information through their hands by touching an object or a person or by using their gut or heart senses and then bringing the energy up to their mind screen to "see." The mind screen is close to the part of the brain connected to the imagination, which we are taught to shut off as we "grow up." So you may question at first if you are "making it up" in your head. That's okay. Over time you will be able to fine-tune the difference and distinguish between the two.

Initially you may see only one color around people. As your ability to pick up different colors in the light spectrum increases, you will be able to see more colors. For example, I saw only clear, purple, or yellow in people's auras for a long time. If this is the case for you, pay attention to the shapes and where they are located. It's valuable information. These were the easiest colors for me to see and connect to initially because my third-eye and solar plexus chakras were the ones I used most.

As I developed a deeper relationship with my root and sacral chakras, my whole visual world opened up. All of a sudden, I could see all the colors of the rainbow. If you want to see vibrant colors, I recommend using the exercise in chapter 6 (see page 166). It is specifically dedicated to grounding your root chakra and also deepening your relationship with your sacral chakra and the emotional layer of your aura.

Practicing with a Friend

Now that you are a bit more familiar with feeling subtle energy in your hands and your aura, it is time to try to see an aura. This is going to take practice and presence. The more present you are in your body, especially in your lower two chakras and aura layers, the better your odds. In the next few sections I will take you through the steps to perceive and see the aura on your mind screen. At first it will be easier to see another's aura. Then you can work up to seeing your own. You will be creating an ideal viewing environment indoors, but after you have practiced a few times, you can then practice viewing wherever you go. Great places to try are in an audience while watching a speaker or presenter on stage, in a park while people watching, or on the sidewalk while walking and viewing the tops of people's heads in front of you. When you have success seeing something, make sure to take note of it. What were you feeling in your body? What layers in your aura felt open or closed? This will help you get back to that place faster in the future.

The more energized and expanded your aura is, the more likely you are to see. Some of the tips from chapters 5 and 6, such as putting on your favorite music and dancing, doing a grounding exercise, or having a good laugh with a friend, are really helpful. Whatever you can do to get your root and sacral chakras open will help with the following exercises.

SIMPLE STEPS TO SEEING ANOTHER'S AURA
Make sure your friend is on board and understands the intention of this viewing exercise. While good intentions are usually implied with friends, the more direct you are, the stronger the joint intention can be. This is the foundation for creating a unified field.

Ask your friend to sit in front of a light-colored wall, preferably white without patterns. Seat yourself about six feet away to make sure you are outside their aura. If there is a specific type of music that relaxes you, feel free to play it during this exercise. Now close your eyes and relax your body as if you were going into a deep meditative state.

I suggest starting with the root grounding exercise in chapter 6 (see page 166). This will allow both of you to expand your fields and create a strong pulsation, which is easier to see.

Once you have grounded and created a deep presence in your body, you can begin to open your eyes. It's important to keep your awareness inward and use soft gazing to view the aura. Imagine you are looking through your friend and that the wall is no longer there. This allows you to use your long-distance, peripheral vision to see. You can rest your eyesight on your friend's forehead, but do not focus on it. Bring more awareness to the outer boundary of your vision.

Wait to see if you feel the pulse of your friend's aura. The pulse is not consistent, so don't be discouraged if it goes away. Keep breathing and wait for it to come back again. What colors do you see on your mind screen? Do this for about 20 minutes and then relax and share what you both discovered.

SIMPLE STEPS TO SEEING YOUR OWN AURA

Seeing your own aura can be a bit more difficult than seeing someone else's. You have become so accustomed to being inside your aura that it may feel counterintuitive to move into a state of surprise and curiosity when viewing yourself. Be open to something new and know that you are constantly shifting from moment to moment.

This exercise is great to do right after or while you are making an energy ball with the exercise earlier in this chapter because you are bringing a lot of energy to your hands. The more attention you bring to the sensations you are feeling, the more you will be able to see.

You can do this exercise seated in a comfortable position. It's easiest to do it with a light-colored or white background. Keep in mind that you will be using the same soft gaze and your peripheral vision, like you did in the exercise with a friend.

Dropping into the sensations in your body and your hands, rub your hands together briefly and, with your palms facing each other, move your hands very slowly closer together and farther apart until you feel the subtle energy or pulsations.

Now place your hands as far away from your eyes as you comfortably can with your palms facing away from you and turn your fingertips from each hand inward so they are close together or touching. See if you can first feel the subtle energy pulsating or connecting your fingers. Then imagine you are seeing through your hands and allow the background to fade away. You can also slowly move your fingertips apart or align different fingertips together to see if you can perceive the energy jumping or moving from around your hands. Sometimes crossing and uncrossing your eyes will help you start seeing the subtle energy around your fingers.

Continue to take long, deep breaths while you do this. Be patient with yourself because it takes time and practice to stay in a relaxed and open state.

Interpreting What You See

It's interpretation time! Feel free to flip back to the different sensations of the aura layers in chapter 1. For help to access and discern different colors and frequencies and the traits they are connected to, refer back to chapter 2. Colors can indicate your current mood or areas where you may be holding energy. You can refer to chapter 3 to help you discern what chakra senses you are using most often or ones you want to develop more.

What did you notice with your other chakra senses while you were viewing yourself or your friend? What sensations in your body were you feeling? Even if you didn't see something, did you pick up other information that was going on with your friend or with you?

It's important to stay curious and open. Don't be quick to define what the information you received means. Moving into an inquisitive state, like a young child, will allow the larger experience to make itself known to you over time. You can use the following items to help home in on your experience.

- **Colors:** What types of colors do you notice? Do the colors move like clouds or pulsate? Is the color stationary? Is it connected to an area in the physical body? Are the colors bright and vibrant or dark and dull?

- **Feelings:** Focus on different parts of your body and imagine they are speaking to you. What do they say? What would happen if you were to respond and have a conversation? Can you offer to meet a need for this part of you? Do you feel like running away or ignoring it?

- **Location:** Where are your eyes naturally drawn to? What is your gut sensing? What is your relationship to this part of your body? Do you feel it shift when you are around different people? What types of people make it feel warm and open or feel tight and uncomfortable?

- **Textures:** Textures are the context of subtle energy. They tell us the what, why, or how. Getting comfortable with recognizing textures gives you information. What sensations do you feel in your hands, feet, and body? Do your hands get warm? Does your heart feel open or full? Do you feel something electrical and cold?

RECORDING YOUR AURA EXPERIENCE

Keep a diary or journal and write down all your experiences while perceiving subtle energy. It is extremely valuable to have your notes all in one place. As you become more comfortable recording your impressions, you build trust in yourself and your ability to track subtle energy. This trust allows the world of subtle energy to become a very tangible experience in your life.

Your guidance and higher self want to develop a relationship with you. Sometimes your impressions will be images your higher self creates to form a mutual language for your deeper understanding of the information. Over time you will recognize certain colors, images, archetypes, and symbols as your personal correspondence with your guidance—a shorthand for you to understand a larger meaning it is trying to reference for you.

Make a key or a legend for the various ways you receive information and create symbols or acronyms for these. You can also use colored pens if you want. This is your journal, so make it your own. It is a playground where you get to develop a strong relationship with how your guidance specifically comes through for you.

Sometimes your impressions will not be about you, but they will be about what you are picking up from the environment and people around you. Once you get to this point, you can start to ask others about your impressions and validate how accurate they really are.

Auras Can (and Do) Change

Your relationship with your aura can change over time with your positive intention to honor your authentic needs and your personal truth of what is right and what resonates with you. Through your relationship with your aura and chakras, you can find an experience of wholeness, which slowly heals you from the inside out. This process, while it takes time and dedication, is a much faster process of healing than trying to change the external world.

It's important to always treat yourself with tenderness, loving kindness, and compassion as you navigate these areas within yourself. The more you can comfort and soothe these areas, the more space you will create in your aura. This will allow darker layers and colors you may encounter in your aura to slough off or dissolve over time, exposing the more vibrant colors underneath. It is helpful to notice that these darker clouds or blocks were created by painful experiences you had and are not to be confused with who you actually are—a soul in a human body, a spiritual being having a human experience.

Aura Photography

Having your aura measured is a great way to get validation of your own higher sense perceptions about yourself and can help you track your progress on your journey for greater self-discovery and healing. It is now possible to have your aura measured with the click of a button and receive an in-depth report detailing all the layers of your aura and much more.

Aura photography has come a long way since its discovery in 1880. Nikola Tesla was the first to show public audiences what became known as the "corona effect," the bluish-purple, magenta, luminous halo with lines of lightning you see when you touch a plasma lamp.

Kirlian photography became globally known in the 1970s after decades of research by Semyon and Valentina Kirlian was published. They enhanced the bioelectric camera, which works by running electric current through a metal plate and then taking a photograph of the corona discharge that appears around the fingertips of a human subject (or, for example, a leaf). Although hundreds of papers were published on Kirlian photography, the field was never standardized and over time was written off as pseudoscience. In the 1980s, Guy Coggins tried to fix this issue by creating the Aura Camera, which is still popular in niche healing circles.

You can typically find a Kirlian photography booth at psychic fairs or small studios around the United States that still take these photographs. While there are vague color descriptions that have been created and ascribed to personality traits for these photos, modern researchers say the most you can discern from them are the shapes and movements that your subtle energy, emotions, and thoughts make in your aura. The colors you see in these photographs are not representative of the colors of the chakras or aura layers as stated in this book. They are a fun novelty item.

WHAT TO EXPECT AND HOW TO PREPARE FOR AN AURA PHOTO SESSION

The process of being photographed is quick. While standing, you place one hand at a time under a dark material that blocks out any light. Then you press each of your fingertips individually on a glass pad while it is photographed. There are a total of 10 compiled snaps, and the results are instant.

Depending on your goals and the information you want to get from your aura photo session, you may want to prepare beforehand. This would include any forms of aura healing and techniques you have been using to strengthen and cleanse your aura. You will want to do these right before or as close to your aura photography session as you can. This will give you the most accurate data on what your aura looks like when you are the most balanced.

You will receive a full report of your findings on the spot, and the practitioner is typically trained to go over the paperwork and graphs with you in detail. They will be able to point out the pertinent information connected to your personal goals and interests.

Conclusion

As you grow more comfortable in acknowledging what you are feeling and perceiving, you will be able to bring these impressions and information up to your mind screen and see more clearly over time. The exercises you learned in this chapter are foundational for seeing your aura and the energy around you. As you continue to come back to them, be open to something new happening each time you do it. The expectation of always seeing the same thing shuts off your ability to be curious and in the moment. Be patient with yourself because sometimes seeing is actually feeling. This is a more valuable way to pick up information because, within the kinesthetic textures of subtle energy, the deeper "why" is revealed. We will discuss how to support the information you are receiving in the next two chapters.

CHAPTER FIVE

AURA HEALING

Now that you have opened up to perceiving and reading energy and colors in your aura, you may be wondering what to do with all the information you have found. In this chapter we will explore how to work with imbalances in the aura. Your internal experiences and the environment around you impact your aura health on a daily basis. We will break down what some of these imbalances look and feel like and give you common, practical tools to cleanse and charge your field, depending on what you need. Using these tools over time will help you create a new baseline of aura health and well-being.

A Deeper Look at
Aura Health

When looking at aura health, it's easiest to break it down into five categories: size, shape, structure, texture, and color.

The size of your aura changes as your vitality changes. It is going to appear smaller and even look shrink-wrapped around your physical body during times of stress, lack of sleep, and sickness or even after traveling or moving. Your aura increases in size with physical movement, excitement or anger, meditation, spiritual awakenings, and epiphany moments.

People have a general shape to their aura that is defined over the course of childhood through the repeated emotions and belief systems they experience long-term. The shape of your aura can and will change over time as your emotions and beliefs about the world change. You may experience defining moments, like the first time you fell in love or looked into your baby's eyes, that literally shape your aura in new ways.

Symmetry and boundaries within the aura have to do with structure. The layers of the aura can be solid like a fortress or be porous. When the chakras and aura layers are open and are similar relationally in shape and size, you will experience harmony and health in your life. Do you have a hard time separating work from personal time? Is it difficult to meet your needs and be in relationship with others? When people have the tendency to hold on to things too tightly or try to control their circumstances, this can cause the structured layers of the aura to tighten and compress, forming clouds in the aura. Healthy structure and boundaries in the aura feel solid and flexible at the same time.

Textures in the aura are full of information and tell a story of what is happening. Does the area feel cold or warm? Full or empty? Tight or soft? Perceiving the sensations in the aura opens you to the interconnectedness between the layers. It helps you discern the greater needs present and how to work with them. Finally, color can shift in vibrancy and saturation as you express yourself and can become darker and grayer in the areas we are not expressing or acknowledging in ourselves.

The Importance of Integration

Most of the pictures we see of the aura and chakra systems are idealized versions of what they could look like in a perfectly healed human with no traumas and no issues. It's like a photoshopped image of a model in a magazine—beautiful to look at but not real. You are a complex and dynamic being with the potential for continuous growth. This means your aura is in constant flux, shifting to accommodate what you are feeling and thinking as well as all your external influences. It does so by opening and closing chakras and shifting energy flow temporarily to help you integrate experiences slowly over time and not all at once. This means your aura is not going to look or feel symmetrical and vibrant all the time, and that's okay.

Sometimes it may be difficult for you to access your feelings, while at other times you may feel hit by emotional waves, as if a tsunami were crashing over you. The intelligence of your body creates a natural pendulum that swings between extremes as it finds new balance. These shifts can be felt instantly, or it can take weeks or even months for you to fully experience the results in your life. Just like with any physical change you make in your body, it's most helpful to look at your patterns over the long term than to judge your aura health by what is happening in the moment.

I've had many clients come to see me over the years, blaming themselves for doing something wrong because they are experiencing physical or emotional pain. Pain is often a reminder to look at an area we have ignored for too long, but you may also experience brief pain or challenges as you revisit old patterns—that is part of the healing journey. Personal and spiritual growth often require us to go back to the original pain so we can solidify what we have learned.

Let's look at the differences between fluctuating integration and signs of imbalance in your aura.

SIGNS OF IMBALANCE IN THE AURA

The longer a repressed emotion or energy block is held in the body, the more disturbance or imbalance is created in the aura. This is because the aura is overcompensating for areas that are being pulled out of alignment, just like when your spine moves out of alignment when your muscles are tight.

When the emotional layer of the field is not expressed, it can become small and dark. The most common signs of repressed emotions are anxiety, low energy, negative mood or depression, and addictive behaviors.

If you are noticing your aura has twists or blocks, it is often a sign that your negative conscious thoughts and unconscious belief systems about the world are disconnecting you from yourself. If it is easy for you to visualize certain colors of your chakras but difficult to see the color in others, this probably means you have a weak connection to that chakra or it is under-functioning.

The most common signs of emotional upheaval, such as grief, are gray to dark gray clouds in the outer layers of the aura. These are the emotions expanding and moving out of the field. It can take time for them to move out. The tools and exercises described later in this chapter can help speed up this process.

Energy Healing is Complementary to Medical Care

Full-spectrum healing happens when you address all the layers of your aura. This often takes a team of dedicated health professionals all holding different pieces of your health puzzle. Aura healing is one of many complementary modalities that can be used along with Western medical treatments.

If you suffer from depression and the medication from your doctor hasn't completely decreased your symptoms, other complementary methods are available and are designed to be used alongside treatment programs to help support you.

It takes time for complementary, emotional, and energetic methods to create physical changes, so it's important to stay on medications and reach out to your doctor for medical care if you are having physical symptoms while you are receiving other care.

HEALING ON EVERY LAYER OF THE AURA

The following table outlines additional healing modalities that focus on specific chakras and layers of your aura. There are resources in the back of this book for most of the therapies mentioned.

AURA LAYER	CHAKRA	COMMON HEALING MODALITIES
Etheric	Root	Conventional and Traditional Chinese Medicine
Emotional	Sacral	Somatic and Humanistic Therapies
Mental	Solar Plexus	Behavioral and Cognitive Therapies
Astral	Heart	Psychodynamic Therapies; Shamanic Healing
Etheric Template	Throat	Singing and Music Therapy; Soul Purpose Work
Celestial	Third-Eye	Kundalini Yoga; Transcendental Meditation
Ketheric Template	Crown	Angelic Healing; Nondual Therapies

INTERNAL CONTRIBUTORS

How you feel and think has a wide-ranging effect on the health and well-being of your aura. Holding in emotions like resentment, guilt, shame, and humiliation is one of the biggest internal contributors to aura imbalance.

Due to painful experiences, we all learn to disconnect from specific areas or layers of our aura to avoid experiencing that pain again. This all happens before the age of reason (usually ages six to nine), so it rarely makes sense to our adult self. This early avoidance typically moves into the subconscious mind, so we become unaware as adults of what emotions, thoughts, false belief systems, and relational dynamics we are avoiding. We then judge ourselves for self-sabotaging, which only compounds the initial splitting and makes it even harder to find the original pain.

When you feel split between only two options, either black or white, it's a strong indicator that you are in an unconscious bind—a blind spot. When you are open and connected, there are always multiple creative ways you can solve a problem.

Working with blind spots is challenging because you can't see them! This is where shadow work and somatic, psychodynamic, and humanistic therapies can play a deeper role in self-discovery and aura healing. Working with your internal imbalances expedites your personal and spiritual growth and heals your aura faster than trying to change or control things outside yourself.

EXTERNAL CONTRIBUTORS

You are exposed to external factors on a daily basis that can drain your energy and make you feel irritable and negative. These could be simple things. For example, working under florescent lights or in front of a computer slowly depletes the chi in your energy field.

Other environmental stressors, such as verbal or physical abuse from others, can cause astral debris to build up in your field. I can see exactly where a person had a bad fall because the outer layers of the aura are disconnected and pushed out in the opposing direction. Broken bones and surgeries also disconnect you from certain layers of your aura and create tears in the field, and scar tissue from surgeries like C-sections can block energy flow through that area of the body. If you have had one of these physical traumas, spend more time bringing energy to these areas.

HOLES AND DARK SPOTS

Dark energy, or colors like black and gray, can mean many different things (see pages 53 and 57). If you are relatively healthy and notice them in yourself or other healthy people, they are most often evidence of repressed or stagnant emotions or energy.

In people who are experiencing long-term chronic pain or a physical disease process like cancer or an autoimmune disease, dark black spots appear deep in the aura and can have a thick, sticky feeling to them. They may also have holes or tears present, which feels more like a vacant, vacuum quality. Tears cause energy to leak from the aura over time and lower the vitality of the person.

Holes or large tears in the aura are not necessarily black. They can be clear in color, or you may see the color of the chakra above or below that area, leaking into that location because the boundaries and energy grids have been broken. Sometimes tears happen from emotional trauma, so there can also be repressed emotions or energy there. This is when you might see dark clouds with varying shades of light gray to black.

You can clear dark energy and clouds using the tools in this chapter. If the dark spot remains or you suspect there might be a rip or tear in the aura, I recommend seeing an experienced energy healer who has been trained in repairing tears in the aura.

Healing Tools

Perceiving and feeling into the subtle energy of your aura is one of the most powerful tools you inherently possess. Much of aura healing is about acknowledging and moving through your internal process work. Some of the contributing factors to your aura health are also external. There are many tools you can incorporate into your aura cleansing practices to support both.

These basic building blocks of aura cleansing and the exercises in this book will help you support yourself through integration and periods of change. They also help expedite the movement of stuck emotions, clouds, and blocks in your aura and charge and rebuild your energy.

When using these tools on another person, it is always necessary to ask the person for permission first. While it may be implied, giving verbal consent before receiving something creates an opening in the aura that allows the person to take in the healing and cleansing on much deeper levels.

SACRED HERBS

For a quick aura cleanse, the smoke from white sage clears the general emotional debris and negative energies in the outer layers of the aura. You will typically find loose white sage pieces bundled together with thread. This makes the sage easy to light, and it will burn for extended periods of time. Make sure to have a ceremonial bowl or seashell handy to catch sparks from the burning bundle and to extinguish it when finished. For stickier, deeper gunk, try swirling palo santo or cedar smoke in specific areas to loosen it over time.

Opening sacred space with smudging is always done counterclockwise, like opening the lid of a container. Closing sacred space is done clockwise, screwing the lid back on with your intentions of what you want to receive. This can be done with the burning of sweetgrass, which is used to attract positive energies and offer sacred prayers and blessings. You can also visualize pure white or gold light entering the space from above.

Incense is often burned as a sign of respect for the divine. This is commonly done in Indian and other Asian traditions as well as in some modern Western religions. It is a way of bookmarking, with respect, the opening of a ceremony or meditation or filling sacred space with the specific energy of the herb. Frankincense is commonly used today, as it has been through antiquity, for religious ceremonies. It has antiseptic and anti-inflammatory properties.

CRYSTALS

Crystals and stones are excellent tools for enhancing the energy of a chakra or strengthening a specific color in your aura. They can cleanse and be programmed to transmit intentions. Allowing yourself to bathe in the energy of a crystal's specific color frequency transmission can be done by wearing it as jewelry, placing it in a bath, holding it in your hands as you meditate, or placing it in a specific place to enjoy its presence.

The following are seven crystals or stones that strengthen the chakras for aura healing:

Black tourmaline is a cleansing and grounding stone. It cleanses the emotional body of negative thoughts, anger, and feelings of unworthiness. It increases physical vitality, reducing stress and tension.

Carnelian opens and creates vibrant connection to personal power, strengthens the emotional body, and helps circulate vital energy.

Citrine strengthens connection to inner sovereignty to stay true to oneself and one's authentic needs. It makes one less susceptible to negative influences. It is quartz, has some cleansing qualities, and can be programmed with your intentions.

Rose quartz transmits the frequency of love, kindness, and purity. Because it is quartz, it holds the personal intentions you give it.

Kyanite opens perception of subtle energies and communication between you, your higher self, and guidance. It balances all the layers of the aura with the physical body.

Charoite is a soul stone that provides strong physical support and strengthens the light body around the aura. It gives clarity of mind by removing unhealthy influences from the psyche.

Selenite vibrates with the pure energy of light and divine consciousness. It clears energy blockages, purifies all chakras, and cleanses energy of other stones and objects. It never accumulates or retains negative energy. You can charge it in the sun, but it never needs cleansing.

ESSENTIAL OILS

Essential oils hold the healing frequencies of plants and herbs. To experience their benefits, apply them directly on your body with a carrier oil like almond, olive, or jojoba. Hydrosols, or aura cleansing sprays, are essential oils added to water. Spray the mist in your aura or in your space for instant cleansing effects. Each oil has specific qualities that can strengthen and balance the aura, uplift or calm the nervous system, and nourish or activate your energy.

The following are five popular essential oils for supporting and cleansing the aura:

- **Cedarwood** is sweet, comforting, and warming. It strengthens confidence and willpower. It brings spiritual clarity while powerfully grounding you into your body. It is associated with the wood element.

- **Jasmine** harmonizes the aura and calms and soothes while opening intuition. It releases fear and is excellent for meditation. It connects the crown and root chakras and is associated with the metal element because it reduces overstimulation of the mind.

Lavender has so many uses that it's the quintessential oil to have at home. It harmonizes all the chakras and balances the aura. Lavender relaxes the nervous system, clears emotional upheaval, and calms the spirit by dispelling anger and heat from the body.

Lemon promotes clarity with uplifting stability. It is nourishing, stimulating, and good for relieving restlessness, anxiety, or suffering from lack of Earth energy. It is associated with Earth.

Peppermint invigorates, energizes, and helps clear headaches. Use it with massages to increase chi flow. It balances the first and fifth layers of the aura for clear communication. Rub it on your feet to bring down a fever. It is associated with the fire element.

MINERAL SALTS

Adding natural mineral salts like Dead Sea, Epsom, Celtic, or Himalayan to your bath is an enjoyable way to cleanse your aura. Each one has distinct qualities. Dead Sea salt is especially sought after because it is composed of over 20 minerals and is high in magnesium without the high sodium chloride all other sea salts have. This gives you all the benefits of clearing inflammation from your body and dark clouds and astral debris from your aura without the drying effects on your skin. Epsom salt is also high in magnesium and is a less expensive way to cleanse your aura with the same great benefits. It is not, in fact, salt. It is actually man-made, crystallized magnesium sulfate but is called salt due to its appearance. Celtic salt is gray-white in color, and Himalayan salt has a characteristic rosy hue due to its wide range of trace minerals. Both are high quality and minimally processed salts that cleanse the aura and offer remineralization, which strengthens chi circulation in the body.

Baking soda is an excellent addition to your bath with the salt of your choice. It alkalizes and softens the water while also having some aura cleansing and detoxifying benefits. One cup does the trick!

Quick Fixes

Sometimes you need an easy go-to for an instant shift to re-center or cleanse your energy. These quick fixes can be used as a daily ritual or to provide a temporary mood or energy booster to get you back in your groove.

RELAX

Find a calming essential oil like lavender or jasmine, put one drop in the palm of each hand with a few drops of carrier oil, and rub your hands together vigorously. Then cup your hands over your mouth and nose and take deep, slow breaths in through your nose and out through your mouth until you feel the effects of your nervous system attuning to the frequency of the scent. You can add an affirmation such as *"I love and accept myself as an expression of the divine."*

ENERGIZE

Put on your favorite music and dance! Dancing is one of the quickest ways to expand your aura and the emotional and astral layers of the field. Pick the type of music that really gets your hips moving or your feet tapping. Dropping your heels on the ground rhythmically opens the root chakra and gets you back in your body. I do this all the time to prepare for client sessions.

UPLIFT

Create a five-minute ceremonial time-out to re-center and uplift yourself that you can use regularly. The simpler it is, the better, and the more you do it, the faster your body will adapt and reset. Utilize multiple senses. Burn your favorite candle and light an incense stick over the flame. Find a short meditative song to play or an affirmation you would like to focus on, such as *I am nourished, nurtured, and supported.* Sit quietly with your breath and allow your awareness to drop like a stone through water down into your pelvic bowl. You can add one drop of lemon essential oil with a carrier oil behind both ears and breathe in the scent.

RECHARGE

Take notice of the places, people, or situations where you constantly feel zapped. Where do you feel it most in your body? What chakras would benefit from some extra energy? Choose an energizing crystal for your specific chakras in need. You can wear it as jewelry or find a tumbler stone to carry in your pocket or purse for when you need it most. There are multiple choices at your local crystal gem shop. My favorites for protection and grounding are citrine and black tourmaline.

CLEAR
Find a space, preferably outside, where you can light your white sage bundle over your ceremonial bowl or seashell. Gently blow on it until you have created billowy smoke. Swirl the smoke around your head, down your shoulders, and down both arms, spending ample time on your hands. Then move it down the trunk of your body, your legs, and your feet and over the soles of your feet. You can end by placing the bowl on the ground with the sage inside, allowing your entire aura to be enveloped with cleansing smoke while stating an affirmation such as *"I release what no longer serves me, and I call in my sovereign expression of the divine"* and feeling light enter and fill your aura from above.

Cleansing the Aura

Cleansing the aura is like taking a spiritual bath. It's important to do regularly to keep our energy vibrant and activated for overall health. How much time do you spend hanging on to little frustrations or agitation during the day? These can become stuck or can stew inside you, bringing down your energy. The more often you cleanse your aura, the less you will have to sit in old emotional gunk. This opens you to receive new and higher energies into your aura.

Beginning on page 138 is a list of exercises I use on a regular basis to cleanse my aura.

Cleansing Your Aura Tools

To cleanse your aura, be sure to cleanse your tools, too. Over time your crystals and jewelry can take on lower frequencies or vibrations in your field, causing the clarity and balance in your aura to drop.

Before cleansing your aura, clear your crystals by smudging them with sage, passing them quickly through the flame of a candle, or placing them in direct sunlight for a good portion of a day.

For your jewelry, make a cleansing and charging station by placing your pieces on a selenite plate or slab overnight. In the morning, create an energy ball with your hands and program an affirmation into your jewelry before putting it on.

AURA CLEANSING BATH

One of the most enjoyable ways to cleanse your aura is by drawing a warm bath at the end of the day. Add all your favorite things, depending on what you feel you need. For extra clearing, I often add up to 4 cups of Epsom salt with 1 cup of baking soda or Dead Sea salt. This will drain a lot of energy from your field, so feel into how much you want to clear at one time. You may want to take it slowly by starting with 1 cup of Epsom salt and working your way up. Also, make sure the water is not so hot that you feel faint afterward. After cleansing your aura, it's always important to recharge. I recommend lying down after a bath and consciously visualizing white light coming into your aura through your feet, hands, head, and chakras for about 20 minutes.

1. Draw a warm bath.

2. Add 2 cups of Epsom salt.

3. Add 1 to 2 drops of cedarwood oil.

4. Add a carnelian tumbler stone.

5. Turn on your favorite meditation music.

6. Soak in the energy for 20 minutes or longer.

Say your healing intention or daily affirmation while you take your cleansing bath.

> *I release that which*
> *I no longer need,*
> *and I openly receive*
> *what is in my soul's*
> *highest alignment.*

7. Lie down and reabsorb energy for 20 minutes. You can hold the carnelian from the bath or choose another reenergizing crystal.

CEREMONIAL SMUDGING AND REACTIVATION

Ceremonial cleansing and reactivation of your home, healing room, or meditation space is a powerful way to reset the energies and manifest more of what you want in your life. Start by tidying up or even reorganizing furniture in a new configuration. Then open all the windows and doors. Light your white sage bundle and continue to fan and blow on it until you have billowing plumes of smoke. Begin by smudging your entire body and aura, paying attention to the soles of your feet and the palms of your hands. Then work your way slowly counterclockwise around the space, fanning the plumes, especially into all the corners. When finished, stand in the center of the space and set your new intention. You can also hold a supportive crystal that has the frequency you would like to infuse into the space.

1. Tidy and reorganize the space.

2. Open all the windows and doors.

3. Light the white sage bundle and smudge yourself and the entire space counterclockwise.

4. Stand grounded at the center of your space and call in a new intention.

5. Hold a crystal to infuse the space with its frequency if you desire.

I release all negative energies that are not for my highest good, and I receive all the blessings the divine has in store for me now.

AURA CLEANSING WITH SELENITE

Use the pure energy of selenite to cleanse and reenergize yourself at the same time. This is nice to do comfortably seated. Center yourself and bring your awareness to your breath. Hold your selenite wand in both hands with your palms facing up. Allow any gray clouds or uncomfortable emotions to slowly drain down your arms into the wand. As you start to feel clearer, begin to connect to the pure uplifting light of the crystal. Then allow this energy to move up into your arms and begin circulating through your body. Use your breath to assist, releasing with the exhale and receiving with the inhale. Do this until you feel your aura is clear of dark colors and you can feel the white light moving through both arms like a circuit. This same exercise can also be done seated with both feet placed on the wand.

1. Comfortably seated, hold the selenite wand with both hands, palms up.

2. Release all clouds and dark energy into the wand.

3. Receive the uplifting energy from the selenite into your arms.

4. Use your breath to circulate the pure energy.

5. State your healing affirmation.

Here is a beautiful affirmation to use with selenite:

> *I love and accept myself as an expression of the divine.*

BURNING EPSOM SALT

Burning Epsom salt with a little bit of alcohol is a smokeless way to powerfully clear astral debris, negative energy, and entities from your aura or from large spaces. It is also odorless, which is great for professional settings when you don't want smoke or the herbal smell of white sage in the air. Pour 1 cup of Epsom salt into a one-liter Pyrex glass bowl with a handle. Lightly sprinkle one tablespoon of any type of alcohol (I use Everclear) over it. It should be barely moistened. Then use a long lighter or match to light the center. The flame will be very high initially and will be a purple-blue color. You may not see it unless the light is turned down. If the flame is bright yellow, it means you added too much alcohol. Sometimes it takes a few tries to find the right mixture. As the flame dies down, you can use a long metal spoon to move the salt around so all of it is burned. State your intention for all negative energy to be taken to the light.

1. Pour 1 cup of Epsom salt into a one-liter Pyrex bowl with a handle.

2. Sparingly saturate the salt with alcohol.

3. Light the salt with a long match or lighter.

4. Use a long metal spoon to shift the salts around so they are all burned.

*I release all
negative energy
to be transformed
into love and light.*

FIRE CEREMONY FOR EMOTIONAL RELEASE

As your aura becomes stronger, it is able to metabolize and let go of old emotions more readily. To aid the release of heavy emotions, you can do a quick fire ceremony. Find a quiet place outside. Bring a tealight candle in a Pyrex glass container or a bowl filled one-third high with water and light it. Connect into your higher self and feel what is ready to be released. Write it down on a small piece of paper and, using your breath, blow all of the emotions into it until you feel you've emptied yourself of the energy. Now burn the piece of paper.

1. Place a tealight candle in a Pyrex bowl or a bowl with water and light it.

2. Connect into your higher self and feel what is ready to be released.

3. Write it down and blow your emotions into it.

4. Using caution, burn the paper.

5. State your healing affirmation.

Repeat as necessary while stating this affirmation:

> *I now release you,*
> *and I receive my*
> *authentic power.*

Conclusion

Honoring the ebb and flow of your aura as it is constantly bringing itself back into balance is a beautiful gift of self-healing. Aura healing is an ongoing practice that you can incorporate into your daily and weekly routines. The more energy work you do, especially if you are a healer practicing on others, the more cleansing you will need to do before and after. It's important for healers to maintain their mineral intake, especially their magnesium and silica levels. Staying open and curious about what you notice in your subtle energy will suggest how often and when these aura healing tools will best support you in coming back into balance.

CHAPTER SIX

STRENGTHENING AND MAINTAINING AURA HEALTH

You have learned a lot about auras, aura health, and how to cleanse and heal your aura. In this chapter you will discover exercises and tools for maintaining your aura health. You will find out how to use your relationship with nature and the elements to recharge whenever you need to. You will also learn how to create a sacred healing space to support your aura cleansing and healing. Practicing the root grounding technique in this chapter will help you strengthen and create symmetry in your aura over time.

Ongoing Aura Health and Maintenance

Now that we've reviewed several techniques to cleanse and heal your aura, it's essential to establish a maintenance program for your aura health. Maintenance involves creating consistency in your daily routines for the exercises and spiritual practices with which you most resonate. Dedicating parts of your day and your week to cultivating a deeper relationship with yourself is the foundation of personal and spiritual growth. It strengthens mindfulness and self-worth. It informs parts of yourself that you are valuable and worth spending time on. This is a meaningful aspect of self-care.

There are so many ways we can become disconnected in the hustle of daily life and caught up in the needs of others or our profession. Choosing to have time for inward exploration is the key to maintaining a powerful relationship with yourself while being open and receptive to others. There are a few simple things you can use in the moment to bring yourself back to center. Compassion and empathy for others keep your auric field open and receptive. Setting aside your own concerns and fears of not getting what you want and just noticing how others are feeling form a simple refrain that will increase the amount of energy circulating in your aura and keep you open to receiving.

We learn to hold on to our stressors and keep them in our bodies. Maybe you've experienced a moment in a professional setting when it doesn't feel "appropriate" to express how you really feel, so you bottle it up. What happens to it by the time you get home? Is it still accessible? If it is, do you give yourself the time and space to let it go? Being honest and open with yourself and doing daily introspective maintenance is a wonderful way to let it go. You can do this by creating a time in the day (in the evenings before bed is a great time) to consciously release anything you pushed down or took on.

This process involves being present with how you are feeling in your body so you know what you need and can give it to yourself in the moment. As you stop allowing the push of your mind to move you forward in life, you will tap into brand-new feelings and areas of human experience.

Tools for Ongoing Aura Maintenance

The following exercises and tools are designed differently from those in chapter 5, which help release discomfort or imbalance so you can experience a positive shift in the moment. The exercises in this chapter are meant to become part of your personal practice and support you over time. There may be a learning curve in the beginning, but as your practice builds, like a snowball rolling downhill, it will give back to you in the long run.

CULTIVATING MINDFULNESS AND PRACTICING GRATITUDE

Whatever we bring our awareness to in our aura, we strengthen our relationship to it. What layers of your aura do you feel need more attention? One of the most common areas we tend to neglect is our relationship with ourselves. Far too often we get caught up in living for the future or worrying about what could happen. This fight-or-flight response disconnects us from the experience of being in the present moment.

Mindfulness is the practice of completely relaxing your body while keeping your mind clear and open, moving you from a "doing" state to a "being" state. Learning how to embody mindfulness allows you to create your life with conscious reflection instead of habitual reaction. Mindfulness techniques have been used for centuries to connect us with one's subtle energy and heal the aura.

One of the most powerful ways we can experience the state of being is through gratitude. Experiencing gratitude is the acknowledgment that life is not happening to us. Instead we are a creator within a larger co-creation, and we are humbled and thankful for this connection and support. It is the ability to surrender and receive at the same time and is one of the most powerfully alchemizing frequencies of the heart.

The simple exercise of sitting down for five minutes and writing as many things as you can that you are grateful for trains your awareness to focus on what is positive and what you are receiving. Try it every morning for a month and notice what transforms in your life.

OPEN TO RECEIVING

What inner voice do you most often hear speaking to you? Is it one that is harsh and judgmental? A problem-solving voice? Does it speak with compassion and understanding?

We all have different aspects within our psyche that can bring a sense of peace and expansiveness or tension, fear, and judgment.

Learning to sit and be open to receiving your higher self guidance—your unique connection with the divine—allows you to dissolve blocks in your throat chakra and the higher layers of your aura. It strengthens your aura so you can become a pure channel for guidance and develops your psychic ability.

RECEIVING GUIDANCE EXERCISE
Find or create a sacred and uplifting place to sit in silence where you will not be disturbed. Choose a simple repetitive ritual to start your session. This could be lighting a candle, burning incense, or listening to a piece of music that brings you into a peaceful mood. Decide how much time you want to spend. You can start with five minutes and work your way up to 20 minutes or longer.

Start with an offering that opens your heart. Think about all the people in your life who have uplifted and supported you. Feel how much you are loved by others and how much you love them. Silently say thank you to them in your heart.

Now slightly switch your vantage point. Bring your awareness to all the synchronicities or coincidences in your life that benefited you in some way. Think of all the things you have been given that you are grateful for that have manifested due to a higher unseen source. Feel the love that source or the divine has for you. Can you fathom it? Silently sit in deep gratitude with the acknowledgment of these blessings.

Sit in silence for the remainder of your time with the intention to receive loving energy and guidance from your higher self. You can imagine this like pure white or golden light coming down onto the top of your head and slowly filling your entire aura. You may hear a loving inner voice speak to you at this time, or you may feel the peaceful transmission in your body. Both are forms of channeling. You can write what you hear or feel in your journal or note what comes to you with a recording device.

Protection

One of the most common questions I receive from my clients is: "How do I protect myself energetically?" This is an in-depth topic I devote a lot of time to in my classes and workshops and is beyond the scope of this book, but I do feel it's important to share some thoughts to reflect on when you feel fear or invasion.

The most valuable tool for protecting yourself is to inhabit your body. When we become frightened or fearful, we lose our connection to our grounding and the lower half of our body. This in turn causes us to think about things we are afraid might happen and makes it harder to know what is real. The more present and connected you are with yourself, the more solid your aura. The more grounded and embodied you are, the stronger your aura becomes. The more open-hearted you are, the less often you take things personally. Keep this in mind the next time you feel overwhelmed or fearful and choose one of the tools in this chapter to keep your aura solid and strong.

DAILY AFFIRMATIONS

As you focus more of your awareness on the gifts and core qualities of your chakras, they will open, increasing your energy to create what you want. You can use these affirmations daily to cultivate your relationship with specific chakras. By spending more time with the areas that feel weaker, you create more symmetry between all the aura layers and develop a healthier aura overall.

Relax your body and come into a state of mindfulness. Speak the affirmation you want to focus on and allow yourself to feel it flowing through you. Sit with the affirmation, using your breath as you speak until you feel completely saturated by your experience. You can create your own affirmations from the aura layer and chakra information in chapters 1 and 3.

Root Chakra:

*I am safe
and supported.*

*My body is strong
and healthy.*

I am abundant.

Sacral Chakra:

*I am enjoying every
moment of my life.*

*I feel safe in my
authentic power.*

*I enjoy the sensations
arising in my body.*

Solar Plexus Chakra:

I trust my perceptions.

*I allow clarity to emerge
before I take action.*

*I am nourished,
nurtured, and supported.*

Heart Chakra:

I am tender and compassionate with myself and others.

I feel a sense of beauty within me and all around me.

I openly receive support from all avenues of creation.

Throat Chakra:

I trust myself.

I allow myself to be an expression of the divine.

I feel safe expressing my truth.

Third-Eye Chakra:

I share what I see with grace and discernment.

I love and accept myself as an expression of the divine.

I open myself to new insights and new forms of expression.

Crown Chakra:

I am a temple of the divine.

What I perceive as challenges are divine lessons of love.

I honor the divine in you as I honor the divine in me.

CONNECTING WITH NATURE

As you learned in chapter 3, the elements are the primary sources of life energy and support for your aura. Creating quality time in your schedule to be out in nature is a supportive addition to your lifestyle that refuels you and rebuilds lost chi from daily stressors. Imagine your energy field as a bucket of water. As long as there is water in the bucket, you are alive. The lower the water gets, the more "drained" you feel. In nature, you absorb the grounding energy from the earth, the prana from the air, and the life-force energy from the sunlight. All of this adds to the amount of chi running through your body—filling your bucket. When you are working under florescent lights or in front of a computer all day, you are draining your bucket.

The following are some great ways to fill up:

- **Gardening, hiking, walking,** and even taking off your shoes and rubbing your bare feet in the grass are enjoyable ways to rev up the meridians and ground yourself into Earth's energy.

- **Waking before sunrise,** between 3 a.m. and 6 a.m., is the prime time to absorb prana from the air. This is a foundational practice for yoga practitioners. It's especially potent when you can be in nature during these early hours. Other breathing techniques, like "breath of fire," can be learned to cultivate your connection to air energy and prana.

- **Walking on the beach** exposes you to healthy negative ions, which increase your body's capacity to absorb oxygen. If you don't live near water, the next best option is to take an Epsom salt or sea salt bath. This is an easy and relaxing way to cleanse your aura and to replenish minerals, like magnesium, through your skin.

- **Getting direct sunlight exposure** revitalizes your energy. Ten minutes of exposure each day before noon or after 3 p.m. has been shown to decrease pain, lighten mood, and increase vitamin D levels. Sunlight accelerates the healing of wounds and is a natural germ and virus killer.

GUIDED VISUALIZATION

There are many meditations and guided visualizations to strengthen your chakras and aura layers. The most valuable one I encourage you to focus on and keep coming back to is the root chakra opening and grounding exercise. So often when my clients jump into this work, they want to "see" and connect to the attributes in their higher chakras right away. They assume that by spending more time in the higher chakras they will obtain those higher qualities faster. This is not the case.

Beginning the work of cleansing and healing requires strength, energy, and space in your aura for all the unwinding that needs to take place. Without it, you may increase the energy in some areas of your aura, but there will not be enough space for the old, unprocessed energy and emotions to move out. Spending even five minutes a day connecting your awareness down through your legs and into the Earth supports all the emotional, mental, relational, and spiritual work above it. Just like the strong roots of the tree support its trunk and branches so it can grow abundant fruit, your commitment to cultivating your relationship with the lower coherent vibrations in your aura supports your entire auric field.

Root Grounding Exercise

Find a place to lie down comfortably or be seated with your feet planted firmly on the floor and open yourself to the feelings and sensations in your body.

Bringing your awareness to your legs and feet, visualize red, thick roots dropping down through your legs, feet, and toes and reaching deep into the rich soil in the Earth. If you live in an apartment building or on land that has been built on top of something else, it may take a little more time for you to feel like you've dropped in or you may have to visualize going down much deeper into the Earth before you find resonate energy to ground into. Take your time and notice your breathing. Your body will relax and open when your roots find their grounding.

As you exhale, consciously begin releasing all toxic thoughts, old emotions, or dark energy down through your roots, allowing the Earth to absorb it. Do this for a few minutes and feel how this release opens more space in your aura for you to receive the Earth's energy up through your root system. With your inhale, feel the Earth's golden-white pulsating energy and allow yourself to drink it up like nectar through a straw. Allow your breaths to cycle with this for a few minutes.

Now allow any intense emotions like anger, rage, jealousy, anxiety, or fear to move down through your roots. Feel how the Earth grounds them and absorbs these frequencies for you.

Continue with this process, allowing your body to match and pulsate with the coherent pulse of the Earth's electromagnetic field and the golden-white star at the center of the Earth. Allow this golden nectar to come up into your feet and legs and fill your entire body. Notice what this frequency of energy feels like in your aura and the sensations it creates in your physical body.

Thank the Earth with deep gratitude for its constant support and open yourself to guidance for developing a deeper relationship with it.

RELATIONSHIP WITH FOOD

Your relationship with food can be a fun way to explore and deepen your relationship with your sacral chakra and the emotional layer of your aura. How much time do you allow yourself to eat a meal? How quickly do you chew your food? What would happen if you allowed yourself to sink in and enjoy the textures and flavors of your food even more than you do now? Your relationship with food is a good indicator of the health of your energy in your pelvis. Food addictions or a lack of desire to eat is connected to our emotions and how we feel about ourselves. If this is an area you feel uncomfortable navigating by yourself, there are many resources and health practitioners who can help open you to the enjoyment and satisfaction that are waiting to be acknowledged.

I do not believe there is a one-size-fits-all diet. Having worked with thousands of clients over the years, I can honestly say that we all have unique ways of resourcing energy. Some auras need more grounding foods, while others can absorb all the energy they need from lighter nourishment. The most important factor to feel into is your experience while you eat and if you feel energized by your meal choices. Eating while in "doing" mode is stressful on your body. Eating while in "being" mode allows your digestive tract to absorb more nutrients and take in more energy from your food. Including a variety of colors in your food choices, staying hydrated, and eating plenty of in-season vegetables and fruits cleanses and nourishes the physical body to support your aura health.

Creating Your Sacred Healing Space

One of the most valuable ways to support your personal healing and maintenance of aura health is by creating an area in your home dedicated to spiritual devotion and your aura cleansing and healing practices. This could be as simple as creating a small altar, designating an area or room for meditation, or clearing the energy of your home. Creating this conscious space for yourself allows you to anchor your intentions so they are constantly being held for you by the objects you have brought into your healing space.

The more energy you give to creating your space and the more time you spend in it, the more it gives back to you. This is a place where you can journal, listen for guidance, do your meditation and breathing exercises, or practice yoga. You may want to look into the energy of the four directions and feng shui when designing your healing space. Other factors to consider are natural light, noise levels, and the types of colors and patterns you would like to surround yourself with. All of these aspects can be utilized to create what you want to manifest in your life.

The following are some objects you might find beneficial to keep in your sacred healing space:

- **Objects** that represent each of the elements earth, air, water, and sun can be placed in your space. This can be fresh flowers in a vase of water with candles and a feather as well as seashells collected at the beach and your essential oils.

- **Spiritual or religious items** help us to connect to our highest experiences of the divine. We each have a unique way of connecting into spirit. Prayer beads or pictures of spiritual icons, saints, and prophets who emulate divine aspects can help drop you into the deeper experiences you are seeking within yourself.

- **Crystals and gemstones** are powerful placeholders of energy. To turn them into placeholders, hold them while breathing your intentions into them or transmitting the color, frequency, or emotion you would like them to hold for you through your hands. Then you can purposefully place them on your altar or around your home to create energy grids.

- **Water** holds energetic imprints, so keeping your essential oils, tinctures, and hydrosol sprays on your altar or next to your crystals and gemstones is a great way to keep them activated.

- **Cards and papers** with your affirmations and other inspirational words are a great way to hold your intentions and bring you back into a state of mindfulness.

- **Photos of loved ones and ancestors** you want to give energy to and receive guidance and energy from can be placed in your space.

- **Ceremonial objects** for cleansing and restoring energetic balance can also be placed in your space. These could include an offering bowl or smudge bowl with a white sage bundle, palo santo, cedar, sweetgrass, or tobacco.

- **Candles** represent the light and the sun and can also be used for clearing the aura. As we experience the release of emotions, we can offer them to the fire and let the flame transmute them.

Conclusion

Each of the maintenance tools in this chapter were included to help you access one or more layers of your aura for strengthening and maintaining steady expansion. Practicing mindfulness and reciting daily affirmations allow your mental layer to be clear, open, and balanced with other layers of your aura. This also brings greater balance between the solar plexus and third-eye chakras. The exercise to sit with guidance and gratitude opens your heart chakra and astral layer and allows the wisdom and knowledge from your higher chakras to come down and integrate with your entire aura, helping you evolve spiritually over time. The grounding and nature exercises will help connect you to your physical body, your root chakra, and the etheric layer of your aura. Broadening your relationship with food is a powerful way to bring yourself into greater enjoyment and satisfaction in your sacral chakra and the emotional layer of your aura. Creating your sacred space with elements and objects that connect you to all the layers of your aura allows your crown chakra to hold space for the divine orchestration of all the aspects of who you are to be in union.

Embracing Our Auras

Through reading this book, I hope that you have discovered specific areas that have piqued your interest and that you can use this book as an introduction to the resources and areas of aura healing you are ready to explore. I suggest picking one or two that resonate most and really diving into those. There are myriad ways to find healing. A technique that works for one person may not work for you. As you advance in your experience of feeling, perceiving, and cleansing your aura, you will be able to track and work with the nuances that arise.

If you don't know where to start, just remember that anything that gets you grounded and in your body is the right foundation.

The most important thing I hope you take away is knowing that anything you do while in a place of mindfulness creates more space and integration within your aura. You could do the same activity, like running, on different days and get different results. Don't get disheartened if you have a challenging day, intense feelings arise, or you have overwhelming experiences down the road. You now have plenty of tools to cleanse the aura and reset.

Create a personal practice with one of the subtle energy movement forms mentioned in chapter 3 or chapter 6. Yoga, Qigong, and chakra meditations and affirmations are strong, long-term foundational supports for your entire aura. They strengthen your ability to slow down and tap into the state of being for increasingly longer periods of time, just like strengthening a muscle. You can gradually train your system to shift into mindfulness like flipping a light switch. I highly recommend finding classes online or near you to support you in growing and maintaining your aura health.

I want you to know that you have access to these self-healing qualities inside you. If you are willing to take the time to listen inwardly and cultivate your relationship with these qualities, you will create a healing response that echoes forth from your soul, not only healing you but also shaping you as a healing transmission for all those you come into contact with.

Resources

Barbara Ann Brennan and the Barbara Brennan School of Healing

BarbaraBrennan.com: The premiere energy healing program in the world for healers to learn their craft in a safe container and learn healthy self-care as a professional healer. Brennan's books *Hands of Light* and *Light Emerging* are classics in the energy-healing field.

Rosalyn L. Bruyere

RosalynlBruyere.org: Author of *Wheels of Light: A Study of the Chakras*, Bruyere is a healer, clairvoyant, and medicine woman. Her significant contributions to energy medicine in the late 20th century make her one of the nation's most successful healers. She teaches in Los Angeles, California.

Science and Nonduality (SAND)

ScienceAndNonduality.com: A forum that brings preeminent thinkers from various scientific fields into dialogue with spiritual teachers, practitioners, and the community at large. Together, they explore deep mysteries and seek answers to eternal questions.

Somatic Experiencing Trauma Institute
TraumaHealing.org: A body-oriented approach to the healing of trauma and other stress disorders created by Dr. Peter A. Levine and based on over 45 years of clinical application.

Dandapani
Dandapani.org: Dandapani teaches simple and effective tools to help you understand and harness your mind.

Institute of Core Energetics
CoreEnergetics.org: Body movement training that allows you to access and release your emotions in a healthy way.

Bringing Your Shadow Out of the Dark and *Spiritual Bypassing* **by Robert Augustus Masters:** These books offer clear boundaries and self-awareness for navigating personal and spiritual growth with compassion for yourself and others.

Eastern Body, Western Mind: Psychology and the Chakra System as a Path to the Self **by Anodea Judith:** An in-depth arrangement of Eastern and Western philosophies with Jungian psychology, somatic therapy, childhood developmental theory, and metaphysics.

Index

Acknowledgments

I wish to thank all my spiritual teachers for their wisdom and for paving the way through embodied transmission for the knowledge within the human energy system to be liberated into mainstream society. I will list them in order as I studied with them: Thank you to Barbara Brennan for giving me the tools to help heal myself from debilitating, progressive illness and for opening me to the healing gifts lying dormant and repressed within me. I am forever grateful to you for showing me how to create the life I never knew was mine to have. To Rebecca Ellens for teaching me what compassionate, embodied, authentic presence looks like in action. To Joy Adler for modeling to me the professional healthy ethics and boundaries of the modern healer. To Jason Shulman for teaching me to receive the ever unfolding, enfolding universe within myself. To Master John Douglas for elevating my soul's path on levels I can't humanly comprehend.

To my husband, Robert, thank you for being my biggest supporter and fan. To my twin sister,

Christa, your honest reflection, unwavering love, and support allow me to see myself clearly and be the best of who I am.

To all my clients who for over a decade have trusted me to hold and reflect you at your greatest depths, I am inspired by the work we do together every day. Sharing this healing work with you gives me tremendous joy and fulfillment.

About the Author

Laura Styler has been in the spiritual and energy healing space for 15 years. Learning from her ancestral healing lineage and the premiere energy healers of our time, she was able to help heal herself from debilitating progressive rheumatoid arthritis and has made it her mission to ignite and awaken the innate healing life force within others to advance global consciousness. She has taught over 1,000 empaths and energetic sensitives how to have their personal power with healthy emotional and energetic boundaries.

Styler holds several degrees in energy medicine, non-dual consciousness, reproductive health, and journalism. She enjoys working with doctors and other complimentary practitioners as part of a healthcare team to enhance the body's natural healing capabilities by repairing rips and what she calls "micro tears" in the human energy field with her surgical-like precision of energy transmission. She is also passionate about helping women through the journey of conscious conception, pregnancy, and post-partum.

Styler lives with her husband in Austin, Texas, and enjoys being out in nature and playing Ultimate Frisbee. She stays busy with her full-time healing practice, Awaken Your Power, and travels throughout the year for teaching and speaking engagements. She maintains continuity of care with her clients via remote healing sessions. More information about Laura Styler's workshops and classes is available at AwakenYourPower.com.

CPSIA information can be obtained
at www.ICGtesting.com
Printed in the USA
BVHW090757171120
593422BV00002B/2

9 781647 398293